The Stories and Secrets of Luton's Medieval Jewel

Katheryne Rogers

© 2000 by Katheryne Rogers
All rights reserved
Published by St. Mary's Parochial Church Council
Scripture quotations are from the
New King James Version of the Holy Bible.
Cover design by Paul Savage
Front cover photo courtesy of Eric Meadows
Printed by White Crescent Press Ltd, Luton
ISBN 0-953-8407-0-0

The author has made every effort to secure permission from copyright holders and apologises for any oversight or error.

Contents

Acknowledgements 4
Introduction 5
1. Before the Beginning 7
2. The Birth and the Brawling 12
3. Toppling Traditions 18
4. Knockdown Punches to the Parish 24
5. Sumptuous Feasts on the Fast Track to Heaven 32
6. English is Hot, Purgatory's Not 51
7. St. Mary's Sun Roof 72
8. Deformities, Destructions and Daniel Knight's Revenge 87
9. The Case of the Missing Vicars 97
10. A Church for All Centuries 121
Appendix A 153
Appendix B 155
Photographic Acknowledgements 158
Notes 159
Index 163

Acknowledgements

I brought no special qualifications to the task of researching and writing *The Stories and Secrets of Luton's Medieval Jewel*, unless it was a deep affection for the ancient parish church and gratitude for the warmth I have encountered there.

Many people took time from their busy lives to encourage and help me with the project. I am indebted to Jennie Gillespie, David Pavey and the Revd Richard Hibbert for their editorial assistance; to Patricia Bell for checking the manuscript for historical accuracy; to Eric Meadows for the kind use of his photographs; to Paul Savage for his artistic abilities and cover design; to Brenton Milne for his instruction on how to tame and subjugate my computer; to Peter White at White Crescent Press for his invaluable assistance; to St. Mary's Vicar, the Revd Nicholas Bell, for his support and enthusiasm; to Lori Lehnherr for proof reading the manuscript; to Rosemary Rodell, Sharon Phyo and Douglas Johnson for their gracious help at the church, and to the Luton Arts Council and Dr. Rebecca Kuhn for their financial contribution towards the publishing.

I'd also like to give a special thanks to Len Ridd, Enid Pearce, Edith Henman, and the Revd Sue Hudspith for their willingness to share their experiences. And to Sandra Hylton, thank you for your friendship and moral support!

Finally, I am grateful to the thousands of people who have attended St. Mary's through the centuries and left us this rich and wonderful heritage.

Introduction

Personally I am not fond of a lot of technical jargon, but as you plunge into the experience of St. Mary's history, a brief explanation of terms might make for a smoother journey.

For instance, the word *advowson* refers to the right to appoint the *rector*, that is, the priest who served the people and received a tenth of all the produce in the parish.

Generally speaking, whoever built a church and endowed it with land, held the advowson. It could not be sold, but the owner could pass it on to his descendents or sign it over to a monastic house, by which act he supposedly shortened his time in purgatory. When St. Albans Abbey obtained Luton's advowson, it took over St. Mary's *rectory estate*. In other words, it received all the tithes of the parish and let the church's land for profit. In turn, the Abbey provided Luton with two priests and kept the church in repair - at least theoretically.

Unfortunately, the system led to abuses, so in the early 1200's certain bishops came up with the concept of *vicarages*. The vicar was a priest and deputy for the monastery, which in turn provided him with a house and a parcel of land from the rectorial land or *glebe*. The vicar's portion of land was referred to as the vicarial glebe. The monastic house still took the highly profitable "great tithes" – a tenth of the produce from the land - while the vicar received the small tithes (ten percent of the garden produce, eggs, cheeses, etc.). The monastery continued to hold the advowson, however, and nominated the next vicar when a vacancy occurred.

This system functioned until the dissolution of the monasteries. At that point, the crown took over monastic properties and sold the rectory estates to individuals and in some cases colleges.

Hence in the late 16th century St. Mary's rectorial tithes landed in the hands of Trinity College, Oxford, and George Wingate of Biscot.

And finally, for informed historians, it might be appropriate to add that in the early chapters, I have primarily followed the stories set forth in Samuel Austin's *History of Luton and its Hamlets* and Henry Cobbe's 19th century book, *Luton's Parish Church*. Some of their statements, particularly regarding manors and charters, conflict with those presented in the Victoria County History.

1.
Before the Beginning

First-time visitors gasp in astonishment as they swerve off the roundabout and suddenly come face-to-face with St. Mary's. Amidst the glut of utilitarian buildings, such an exquisite piece of architecture is startling. But the pride of Luton, St. Mary's Parish Church, is a medieval jewel that has been capturing attention for over 800 years. People passing by may appreciate the building or be curious about what goes on inside. Few are aware that the church houses a treasure of tantalising stories and secrets.

A chapel financed with ransom money? A wealthy Vicar who wound up a beggar? Why were three fire engines parked inside the church? Why were members of the congregation sleeping with the church silver?

St. Mary's has a dashing history and can boast of her connections to kings, queens, crusaders and knights. She even has ties with historical figures in America. Conversely, criminals are also in her closets.

The story of St. Mary's actually begins before a church was consecrated on the present site in 1137 AD. The congregation gathering in the new stone edifice had simply moved from one building to another. Their ancestors had worshipped in yet another. They were the same church, however, with roots reaching back almost to the beginnings of Christianity in Bedfordshire, when the royal town of Luton[1] was part of the Kingdom of Mercia.

Our story opens around the year 653 AD:

"I wish to marry your daughter Alhflaed," declared the Prince of Mercia, kneeling confidently before Northumberland's King Oswy. The marriage had been previously arranged, and this request was part of the ritual.

"Paeda, you and your people are pagans. How can I permit such a thing?" Oswy asked, noting with satisfaction the Prince's alarmed expression. This was not according to the script. Before Paeda could protest, however, Oswy continued.

"Yet you are a noble youth, and I will give you my daughter on one condition: you and your Kingdom must accept the Christian faith and be baptised. Are you willing?"

Relieved, Paeda agreed to the terms and went through a period of instruction in the Faith.

"I am ready to become a Christian, and will do so even if the maiden is denied me," he announced after hearing about God's promises and the hope of heaven. Paeda was baptised by Bishop Finan of Lindisfarne, and then journeyed home with his new bride. He also brought back four priests to evangelise and instruct his subjects. Nobles and commoners alike came in crowds to hear these men preach, and consequently accepted the Faith and were baptised.[2]

Of Wood, Wattle and Zeal

After only three years of marriage, "Mrs. Paeda" murdered her husband (one wonders about the thoroughness of her conversion!), but by then Bedfordshire was well on the way to becoming

Christianised. Paeda's brother Wulfhere, a staunch Christian, succeeded him as King.

Wulfhere had a passion for building churches and tradition has it that around 673 AD he provided Luton with its first, situated in the area of Biscot. Making a generous donation from his royal estate, he endowed the church with 600 acres (or five *hides*) and a house. Winfred, the Bishop of Mercia, most likely stayed there when travelling throughout his enormous diocese. The name Biscot evolved from *Bishopscote*, meaning "the Bishop's cottage."

There is no record of what this first church looked like, but it was probably constructed of wood and wattle and topped with a thatched roof. The materials might seem at odds with her wealth, but they reflected the style of the time, as well as the lack of stone in the region.

The proceeds or *living* from the church's lands supported the Bishop and clergy who evangelised, baptised and instructed the King's subjects. Christians were fervently committed to evangelism during this period, so it is not surprising that resources were dedicated to this end.

Monks in particular shook pagan society by their blazing joy and commitment, coupled with a radical departure from materialism. Their powerful testimony reached even into palaces, motivating kings and queens to renounce their thrones and riches to join the monastic life.

As England became Christianised, however, much of this zeal passed away with those early generations. Instead of renouncing their lives and possessions to serve God and mankind, the future rich and powerful came to see the Church – including St. Mary's – as a means of furthering their earthly status.

In 680 the huge Diocese of Mercia was divided, and Luton became part of the Diocese of Leicester. The association with Leicester continued until 1075, when Luton became part of the Diocese of Lincoln.

Nearly all churches were associated with monasteries or collegiate bodies, and Luton's church also passed into the hands of an abbey. History does not reveal which one, but does tell us the name of the Abbot responsible for losing the church's endowment. In the late 700's, Abbot Alhmund made the unfortunate error of offending King Offa. Landowners had to provide the King with one fully equipped soldier for every five hides of land they possessed. Alhmund, in control of the church's five hides, was derelict in his duty. To pacify King Offa, the Abbot gave him the church's lands at Biscot.

The King was pleased. Having recently founded St. Albans Abbey (791), he was able to present the new Abbot with a generous gift of 600 acres and a church in Luton.

Luton's church continued her association with St. Albans until the latter part of the 9th century, when the Danes invaded and severed the tie. Part of Luton fell into Danish hands around 878 as a result of the Danelaw. Norsemen had the habit of destroying churches, and if Luton's church stood on their side of the boundary, it probably did not survive.

A Royal Gesture

Either during the Danelaw or shortly afterwards King Edward began constructing a new stone church near the current site, probably in the vicinity of Park Square. Edward's successor, Ethelstan, completed the church, which was consecrated in 931 AD. Ethelstan was likely aware that the original church endowment was 600 acres, and he bestowed the same amount. The land – probably in the area of Dallow – was the second largest endowment of an English church in Saxon times.

The record of Luton's church is sketchy for the next 100 years, but the reign of Edward the Confessor gives us our first identifiable clergyman. His name was Morcar, and he was the church's last Saxon priest. The people of Luton knew him not only as their priest but also as the third most important person in town.[3] Evidence suggests he was related to Earl Morcar, brother-in-law to King Harold.

Morcar the Priest was a wealthy landowner, possessing not only the 600-acre endowment, but also 75 acres of woodland in Luton, 120 acres in Potsgrove, 60 acres in Battlesen and the church at Houghton Regis with its 60 acres. He also owned a water mill near the church.

During his tenure as priest, the parish contained between 700 and 800 people.

Change for the church came with William the Conqueror in 1066 AD. The Conqueror replaced Morcar with his Chamberlain, also named William, giving him the church and endowment. Tradition has it that either he or his son lived in the manor house at Dallow.

When the Conqueror dispatched men to survey his newly acquired country, they recorded of Luton:

> The Church of this Manor is held by William the King's Chamberlain with the five hides of land which belong to it. These five hides are counted in the thirty hides of the Manor...The church yields 20 shillings yearly. There is woodland to feed 50 swine. The whole was valued in King Edward's time and at the Conquest, and is valued still at 60 shillings. This Church with its land Morcar the Priest held in the year that King Edward was alive and was dead.[4]

Sixty shillings does not sound like much, but it was no small sum for an 11th century church. Further wealth was added before the end of the first millennium, when the church gained a monetary interest in the weekly market and annual fair. Unfortunately, wealth and trouble are often a package deal, as Luton's church was about to find out.

2.
The Birth and the Brawling

When Henry I, youngest son of the Conqueror, ascended the throne, he automatically became lord of the manor of Luton. At Christmas time in 1115, he travelled to St. Albans for the dedication of the rebuilt monastery. In a fitting gesture, Henry bestowed the manor of Biscot on the Abbey, King Offa's original gift lost in the Danish incursion.

King Henry made another generous gift around 1121, when he turned the manor of Luton over to his illegitimate son, Robert Earl of Gloucester. Henry had a number of illegitimate children and provided well for all of them. Like Wulfhere before him, the Earl of Gloucester was a builder of churches and set about building Luton a new one on the present-day site, dedicating it to *St. Mary*.

Prior to constructing the new building, Robert had received the advowson from his father. The advowson brought with it a financial benefit as well as the power to appoint Luton's priest. The King's gift, however, ignited a bitter conflict with William the Younger, son of the Chamberlain. William protested that the advowson was part of his inheritance as long as he provided the Earl with a fully equipped soldier. Earl Robert responded that the church lands donated by Ethelstan were given in free alms and not as a military fief.

Hijacking the Church

Robert tried to resolve this touchy matter in 1130 AD by granting the advowson in free alms to a relative, Gilbert de Cymmay. Cymmay was a clergyman and one of the King's chaplains. But this move only added fuel to the fire. Incensed, William the Younger violently took possession of the old church and ignored repeated summons to appear before the Bishop to prove his case.

The King stepped into the fray at this point. He charged the people of Luton to investigate the church's history regarding the original terms of the endowment. Lutonians reported back that the church had always been held in free alms until William the Chamberlain took control of it.

Robert Earl of Gloucester

Not until two years after the dedication of St. Mary's did the Bishops meet at Oxford and settle the dispute. They awarded Gilbert de Cymmay possession of the church and its lands.

In spite of his conflict with William over the advowson, the founder of St. Mary's had a sterling reputation. One of his contemporaries, William of Malmesbury, dedicated his *History of the English Kings* to the Earl. Regarding Robert he wrote:

> For if any man was truly noble, you certainly excel in that quality; being descended from the most glorious kings and earls, and resembling them in your disposition. From the Normans, therefore, you derive your military skill; from the Flemings your personal elegance; from the French your surpassing munificence...So devoted are you to literature, that though distracted with such a mass of business, you yet snatch some hours to yourself for the purpose either of reading or of hearing others. The fame of your justice reaches even our parts; for a false sentence has never been extorted from you, either by elevation of rank or by scantiness of fortune. Your munificence and disregard of money is amply shown by the monastery of Tewkesbury; from which, as I hear, you not only do not extort presents, but return its voluntary offerings. Indeed, the greatness of your fortune has made no difference in you, except that your beneficence can now almost keep pace with your inclination....Men of learning find in you manners congenial to their own; for, without the slightest indication of moroseness, you regard them with kindness, admit them with complacency, and dismiss them with regret.

Effusive praise certainly, but not unwarranted. Historians speculate that Robert could have been King had he aspired to the position. But a sense of loyalty to his half-sister Maude, the legitimate heir to the throne, eclipsed any desire for power.

What kind of church building did the Earl give us? The original St. Mary's was probably similar to other Norman churches of that period: cruciform in shape, consisting of a chancel, nave, short transepts and a tower where the two intersected.[5] The building was made of stone and dedicated in 1137AD. A corbel from this building can be found today next to the south door.

It was a wretched period for England due to power struggles over the throne. In the year of St. Mary's consecration, the Anglo-Saxon Chronicle recorded:

Corbel from Earl Robert's Church

> Never did a country endure greater misery...and men said openly that Christ and his angels slept.

The new church must have been a source of encouragement for Lutonians in an otherwise bleak time.

One battle for control of St. Mary's had been resolved, but a subtler one was brewing. Although St. Albans possessed the manor at Biscot (the church's original lands), Abbot Robert de Gorham had his eye on St. Mary's current endowment.

Sixteen years after he received the advowson, Gilbert de Cymmay developed dropsy and was presumably near death. Abbot de Gorham became solicitous, demonstrating a touching concern by frequent visits to the sick priest. In the end, he persuaded Cymmay to sign over the church lands to Geoffrey, the Abbot's nephew.

To everyone's surprise, Cymmay recovered. What happened next may have been the result of a deathbed bargain with God or the fact that he was now redundant and without means of support. In any case, Gilbert and his son (he was a married priest) became monks at St. Albans. Geoffrey in turn, became the priest at St. Mary's.

Pinching St. Mary's endowment was not going to be *that* easy, however. Ensuing political changes cast doubt on the legality of the transfer to Geoffrey. In 1154, Abbot de Gorham sought out William Earl of Gloucester (son of Robert and current lord of the manor) and offered him 80 marks to transfer St. Mary's and its lands to the monastery. William agreed, and the tireless Abbot hurried off to get King Stephen's approval, an annoying but legal necessity of the day.

Pilgrims and Profits

What of the congregation at St. Mary's during all this politicking? A decree from the Pope required them to make an annual pilgrimage to the Shrine at St. Albans. Pilgrimages were intended to help their souls, but it can also be argued that they perked up the monastery's moneybox. Parishioners brought offerings and purchased lead badges as souvenirs to prove they had made the journey.[6] In return, they received an indulgence that promised to reduce their time in purgatory.

When King Henry II ascended the throne in 1154, he decided to take back all the royal lands that had once belonged to the crown. This included St. Mary's endowment, and as a result, Geoffrey's two clerks, Balderic de Sigillo and Adam, were dismissed. Geoffrey alone remained to minister to the large parish.

One can only imagine the Abbot's exasperation at losing St. Mary's after all his work to gain it. Apparently he did not lack that godly quality of perseverance though, and two years later he convinced the King to return the lands to the Abbey. Luton's church was one of St. Albans most valuable assets. The advowson implied almost complete control over both the church and its possessions. Profit from the church's income *in theory* went to support two priests at St. Mary's, as well as provide for travellers, guests and pilgrims to the Abbey's shrine.

Near the end of the century, King Richard the Lionheart inherited Luton Manor upon the death of his father in 1189. A year later he sold it to Baldwin de Bethune, a crusader who fought with Richard at Acre in Palestine.

Shortly after buying the manor, Bethune got into a dispute with St. Albans Abbot, John de Cella. The issue was over who had the rights to the profitable market stalls at Luton's annual fair. The conflict was resolved and the resulting document read:

> Baldwin de Bethune, Earl of Albemarle, to all the faithful as well present as future, greeting. Be it known unto you that there was a controversy between me and John, Abbot of St. Albans, concerning the fair of Luton which is held at the Assumption of the Blessed Mary, and concerning the stalls which the Abbot's men had, and the liberties which they had…I however, have ascertained by my men and by the neighbours that the aforesaid fair ought to be the Abbot's on whatsoever day the feast of the Assumption shall fall, except the sale of gold, and of horses, and of tanned hides, and of men who of old were sold, and that the Abbot shall have sufficient stalls and two chests and one shop in the market, and that as to the men of the Abbot they shall have all the liberties which they possessed when the manor was the King's. …And if perchance the market shall be moved to another place, or in anywise changed, I will assign to them just so many stalls in convenient places.

Abbot John was fortunate that the Lord of the manor was so fair-minded. The next century would usher in one notorious for his cruelty and abuse.

3.
Toppling Traditions

The year is 1200, and Sunday Mass at St. Mary's is nearly over. There are no chairs or pews, and your legs are beginning to ache from standing and kneeling. At least rushes on the floor offer some cushioning from the cold stone. The thought of leaning on a pillar is tempting but last week Vicar Roger de Luton warned the faithful not to slouch against the walls or pillars.

It is frigid enough to see the priest's breath as he intones the liturgy at the High Altar. While he carries out his duties up front, parishioners kneeling in the nave recite the Pater Noster and Ave Maria to themselves in Latin, though they do not understand the language. Suddenly the tinkling of a bell announces the high point of the service, when the bread is changed into Christ's body. Everyone cranes to see the Eucharistic bread, which the Vicar holds high.

After the priest's final blessing, people pour out of the church and weave through the crowded market stalls in the churchyard. On this Sunday, like all others, business is brisk.

Yes, as strange as it seems, the market was held on Sundays *in* the churchyard! Although King Ethelstan had prohibited Sunday markets, Lutonians took no notice. The market had always been held in the churchyard on that day of the week. Then William the Conqueror legalised Sabbath shopping, putting Luton back on the right side of the law.

Parishioners from the 1200's would probably feel comfortable in St. Mary's today...aside from the luxury of chairs, that is. Upon walking out the north door, they would immediately see the Arndale Shopping Centre, also open for business on Sundays!

Be that as it may, Baldwin de Bethune, crusader and lord of the manor, found the practice unseemly. In 1202, he changed the market day to Monday. How the citizens reacted is unknown, but King John was miffed. One simply did not make changes without his permission. Consequently, Earl Baldwin was fined for his transgression, although the court upheld Monday as the new market day. After all, it was simply a matter of doing things through the proper channels.

While successful in exercising sovereignty over his nobles, King John ran into trouble with Pope Innocent III. A squabble over an appointment to the See of Canterbury ended in 1208 with the Pontiff excommunicating King John and placing England and Wales under an interdict. For six years the doors of St. Mary's remained shut. In spite of the fact that parishioners could not take communion, get married in the church or be buried in consecrated ground, there are no indications that people were greatly disturbed by the interdict. The only two sacraments permitted by the Pope were baptism and last rites.

If Pope Innocent was depending on Englishmen to overthrow their Sovereign for the sake of their souls, he was disappointed. Churches were not reopened until political expediency motivated King John to be reconciled with Rome in 1214.

A Wicked Brute

Standing in stark contrast with the piety of Earl Baldwin was the wickedness of Falk de Breauté, who came into possession of the manor of Luton in 1216. Breauté stole land, plundered abbeys, killed a monk at St. Albans, and oppressed people simply because he had the power to do so. He despised the Church and its clergy, and St. Mary's did not escape his contempt.

Sometime around 1221, Breauté dammed the river Lea between the vicarage and his castle to the south of the churchyard. The ensuing flood damaged church fields, crops and houses. When the Abbot's messenger complained to Falk, he retorted, "I am sorry I did not wait until the corn had been housed that the water might have destroyed it completely."

But while evil flourished in the form of Falk de Breauté, God was raising up a champion for St. Mary's. Hugh Wells, the Bishop of Lincoln, was disturbed that monastic houses were enjoying revenue from their parish churches while neglecting the spiritual welfare of parishioners. St. Albans for example had reduced Luton's church to a single temporary priest with no legally assigned income. His tenure at St. Mary's depended entirely on the Abbot's whim.

Around 1220, Bishop Wells succeeded in forcing St. Albans to establish a permanent vicarage at St. Mary's. The change meant that the Vicar's living would now come from his parishioners' tithes and offerings, as well as the revenues from the chapels belonging to the church. A house and garden rounded out the package. Luton was among the first of such legally established vicarages in England. The new arrangement also meant that St. Albans surrendered some of its control over St. Mary's.

Luton's first perpetual Vicar was a priest named John de St. Alban. Some sources claim that the purbeck marble font still in use today was a gift from John de St. Alban. Although it makes a nice story, Nikolaus Pevsner, the well-known authority on English architecture, claimed that the font was from the 14th century.

In 1226 Falk de Breauté died, to the relief of everyone, including his wife who insisted she had been forced to marry him against her will.

As St. Mary's increased in age, so did her dimensions. Not long after John de St. Alban became the first perpetual Vicar, aisles were added to the nave and the chancel was lengthened. Increasingly elaborate rituals partly explain the additions. A larger chancel accommodated a greater number of clergy, while aisles permitted them to make processions around the church. Some materials from the old structure were re-worked into the new, and Robert Grosseteste, Bishop of Lincoln, consecrated it in 1228.

The 14th century font erroneously attributed to John de St. Alban.

The Vicar Who Went Begging

Adam de Biscot was Vicar when the consecration of the new building took place. He served St. Mary's for nineteen years before leaving to become a Dominican *friar preacher*, as they were called. Itinerant evangelists, they travelled from town to town ministering to the poor and outcast. The presence of these brothers must have caused discomfort among the ecclesiastical establishment, many of whom were preoccupied with wealth and power. The Friars' reputation was that:

> They cared nothing for material things; they were under vows not to heed the flesh and its temptations. Protected by these vows they went barefoot throughout the world healing sore hearts and mending broken faiths.

In renouncing his position at St. Mary's, de Biscot exchanged a well-cushioned life for the humble existence of a barefoot beggar who travelled around telling people about the love of Christ. The Vicar's radical departure from materialism and commitment to evangelism echoed that of his early monastic predecessors.

A Vicar named Henry took over when de Biscot left St. Mary's. Little is known about him or his successor, Geoffrey. Henry stayed less than a year at St. Mary's, while Geoffrey's tenure, which began in 1248, lasted until his death twenty-seven years later.

Roger de Mursle, the next Vicar, lived only a year after his institution. Hugh de Baneburgh came to St. Mary's in September 1276 to replace Mursle. Three years later, Baneburgh had the distinction of hosting the Archbishop of Canterbury, John Peckham, when he visited Luton.

Simon de Montfort, famous for the first attempt at a representative parliament in England, became associated with Luton in 1238 when he married Eleanor, Countess of Pembroke. The Countess was a widow who had inherited the manor at Luton from her husband. Before meeting de Montfort, she had made a solemn vow to live the rest of her life in celibacy. Such vows were not lightly taken nor easily reversed, and de Montfort was compelled to go to Rome to obtain a papal dispensation. The Pope dispensed, but suggested the Earl go on a crusade to the Holy Land as penance, which he did.

While Simon de Montfort was not intimately involved in Luton, he was favourably inclined towards St. Mary's. In a refreshing gesture, he stipulated that *all* the tithes from his lands in Luton be given to the Church,[7] as opposed to the common practice of deducting a collecting fee.

Thieves Who Arrived at Church on Time

If de Montfort was fond of St. Mary's, so were thieves! Churches in general were attractive for their expensive ornaments as well as the haven they provided from the law. If a criminal could get to a church before being apprehended, he could claim sanctuary. His life was guaranteed, though he was banished from the country.

St. Mary's provided such sanctuary on two occasions in the mid-1200's. In both instances, the prisoners escaped from Simon de Montfort's jail in Luton and fled to St. Mary's. De Montfort was consequently fined for not having a better jail.

One of the escaped prisoners was a woman charged with stealing cloth. Beside the fact that she made it to the church, the only other surviving detail is that she was *Joan, daughter of Emma*. The other accused thief was a man named Gilbert le Fleming. It would not be the last time thieves were found in St. Mary's.

4.
Knockdown Punches to the Parish

You could hardly pick a worse century to be born than the 1300's. Every period has its hardships, but this era delivered one gruelling blow after another to St. Mary's parishioners.

Imagine you had been born in 1320, grew up and married in the church. You remember walking to Sunday Mass as a child and being fascinated with the partially constructed church tower.

"When are they going to finish it?" you would ask from time-to-time. But after a while you stopped asking. Now in 1380 you are sixty years old and the tower is still incomplete. Would it fall into ruin before it was ever finished?

Progress on the tower ceased in the early years of the century when funds ran out. Other renovations underway in St. Mary's also ground to a halt. Blame it on six consecutive bad harvests which impoverished the citizens of Luton. The situation was so desperate that some starved to death. It hit Luton especially hard in 1314, and the following year was the worst known famine in the history of Europe.

Whether or not these conditions had anything to do with the resignation of Hugh de Baneburgh is not clear. But after nearly 40 years as Vicar, he was probably ready to retire anyway. In 1316, Baneburgh turned the position over to Mag. John de Wilden. His title, *Magister*, the Latin word for Master, was a term of respect for someone with academic qualifications.

More hardship followed. In 1317, a disease struck the cows and sheep. It was the Mad Cow crisis of the era, and people ate horsemeat until the danger passed.

The famine and disease may explain why in 1321, the newly installed Vicar, Robert Wyboldeston, owed his creditors £100, or approximately £28,000 in today's money. The debt was levied on his lands in Luton, which may account for the transfer of the living that year to Roger de Salesbury.

Salesbury stayed in Luton 10 years before exchanging to Eversholt. John de Standfordham came to Luton as the new Vicar, but little is know about him except that he suffered from ill-health. John Hanck of Stretley was appointed as an assistant Vicar to help Standfordham because he *works under such great weakness of body*.[8]

Luton was in for still more suffering. In 1336 a fire swept through the town, destroying the wooden houses and shops. Hundreds of families were left homeless, and recovery was slower than a snail's pace. Four years later two hundred homes remained uninhabited and 720 acres of land uncultivated. Even the taxman was impressed and gave Lutonians a rare dispensation until they were back on their financial feet.

St. Mary's herself was untouched by the fire. For at least a while the partially constructed tower harmonised with the rest of the town, in various stages of rebuilding.

There was also the matter of a temporary wall blocking off the chancel since the early 1300's. The church had become a frozen construction site. After so many years, did parishioners give up hope of completing the work?

Disease and Discord

In 1348 the plague struck. When it worsened in 1349, St. Mary's lost three vicars in succession. John de Luton and his successor, Andrew Power de Mentmore, probably both died of the plague. Richard de Rochele, who replaced de Mentmore, only stayed a few months. By this time the pestilence had decimated the clergy, and qualified men were in short supply.

A further complication arose when the Abbot of St. Albans died. Under normal conditions he chose the Vicar for St. Mary's. Instead, King Edward III took it upon himself to appoint a clerk in Deacon's Orders, William de Chaumbre of St. Neots.

The Bishop of Lincoln, however, was displeased by the King's interference and tried to have William de Chaumbre removed. Edward warned the Bishop to back off, but he was not a man easily dissuaded. He merely changed tactics, accused William of certain crimes and deprived him of the living. Every member of St. Mary's probably had an opinion on the subject, even if they did not have a say in it.

Soon a new Abbot was appointed at St. Albans. Thomas de la Mare was quick to realise that his role had been usurped by both the King and Bishop. He immediately rectified this by appointing his choice for Vicar, John Lybert. William de Chaumbre appealed to the ecclesiastical courts, which ruled in his favour and ordered the living of St. Mary's returned to him.

Specific details of what followed are lost in the mists of time, but in 1353 a further conflict arose between the Crown and Abbey that may have been related to this dispute over the Vicarage. Certain individuals bound themselves by an oath and took possession of St. Mary's, half-built tower and all. The King appointed a commission to investigate the situation, but how long they held the church and whether or not services were disrupted is not recorded.

Through it all, St. Mary's continued to look like a construction site. The plague not only left a shortage of clergy, but the ranks of labourers were decimated as well. Even if funds existed to finish the renovations and tower, there were few skilled workers. At least one-third of the population of Luton died. St. Albans Abbey was particularly hard hit. Forty-seven of the monks, approximately 85% of the community, succumbed to the sickness.

In the latter part of the 1360's, a priest named Benedict de Massingham decided he wanted to be St. Mary's next Vicar. Rather than making his request directly to the Abbot of St. Alban's, he took an underhanded route and convinced the University of Cambridge to petition Pope Urban V on his behalf. While the petition was granted at Avignon on 27 September 1366, Massingham never made it to St. Mary's for some unknown reason.

Aside from the terrible disasters of the century, a bitter struggle persisted between the Abbey and its tenants. The tenants felt misused and objected to the Abbey's monopoly of the corn mills. Hostility and violence against the monastery erupted throughout the century, culminating in King Richard II bringing an armed force to St. Albans in 1381 to restore order. Eighteen troublemakers were hung, but the situation remained volatile. Arson and destruction of manor houses and Abbey goods continued throughout the century.

Survival issues superseded the reconstruction of St. Mary's, yet sixty years of abandoned needs must have been disheartening for the parish, if not a source of shame. The half-built tower was a looming accusation that men had neglected Christ and His church.

John Wycliffe certainly thought so. An ordained clergyman in the same diocese as St. Mary's, Wycliffe began denouncing the clergy around 1375 for taking so much from the people and giving so little in return. He wrote:

> Pride and covetousness of clerics is the cause of the Church's blindness and heresy, and deprives them of the true understanding of scripture.

Wycliffe also abhorred the fact that people could not read the Bible in their own language and were at the mercy of whatever their priests taught them. To remedy this, he and his followers translated the Scriptures into English and in so doing, drew even more hostility from the ecclesiastical establishment. The Abbot of St. Albans had copies of Wycliffe's Bible publicly burnt. He also warned St. Mary's Vicar not to have anything to do with Wycliffe and his Bible.

The Wealthy Say it With Wax
In 1377, while Wycliffe was preaching against church practices, William Wenlock came into possession of one third of Luton Manor and was appointed Master of Farley Hospital. He was also a Canon of St. Paul's Cathedral. His will, dated 1 April 1391, stated that:

> He wishes to have 5 candles each of 20 lb. of wax around his body on the day of his burial and in the same way 12 suitable torches…He wills that 12 poor men shall carry the said 12 torches…On the day of his burial 100 shillings is to be distributed among the poor so that there is 1d.[9] for each. [10]

No doubt an impressive funeral! Wenlock also paid for 100 Masses to be said on the day of his death and another 100 on the day of his burial. Furthermore, he left money for the singing of a number of Masses for his soul at both St. Paul's Cathedral and Westminster Abbey.

These Masses were intended to expedite the soul through purgatory. The poor who received money from the deceased were expected to pray for his soul as well.

William Wenlock's tomb is located under the Wenlock Screen, next to the chancel. He is represented by the figure of a priest holding a rosary and wearing robes that were originally painted scarlet.

Two inscriptions are engraved along the edges of the tomb. The inscription facing the chancel is in Latin and translated reads:

William Wenlock

> This William here in earth,
> At Wenlock had his birth,
> Priestly were his order's worth.
> While he lived, of this fair town,
> As a Lord he bare renown.
> Though unworthy here he lie,
> May God receive his soul on high.

Facing the chapel side of the tomb is an inscription in old English, thought to be one of the earliest English epitaphs in the country. It reads:

> In Wenlock brad I: in this toun lordscipes had I:
> Her am I now fady: cristes moder helpe me lady:
> Under thes stones: for a tym schal I reste my bones:
> Deye mot I ned ones: myghtful god gran'nt me thy wones. Ame.

During the time William Wenlock resided at Farley Hospital, the Vicar at St. Mary's was Master Walter Ixworth. Almost nothing is known about him, including the year of his institution. It is also unclear whether he succeeded William de Chaumbre or John Lybert, since history fails to record which of those two finally served as St. Mary's Vicar.

The Revd John Peche, LL.B. was instituted at St. Mary's in 1393. He was the first to hold a University degree above the ordinary degree of Master of Arts.

New Fashions and Furniture

Thankfully, the terrible thirteen hundreds ended on a positive note. A number of considerably wealthy men living in Luton contributed to the costs of completing the tower and other partially finished renovations. The great arches at the crossings were erected, the transepts enlarged and the Someries and Hoo Chapels added. The ground floor of the vestry adjoined the chancel and a crypt beneath was constructed. The rood loft and screen were erected and a large crucifix hung from the screen. The Easter Sepulchre on the north side of the altar was constructed at this time as well.

The 14th century baptistry

Crowning the new additions was an elaborately carved stone baptistry. Tradition claims that Queen Philippa gave it to the church around 1340 to encourage the citizens of Luton in the aftermath of the fire and plague. Unfortunately, no records exist to prove this one way or the other.

Meeting in their freshly renovated building at the close of the century, parishioners probably couldn't help feeling that more prosperous times lay just ahead. They were not to be disappointed.

5.
Sumptuous Feasts on the Fast Track to Heaven

Parishioners hurrying towards St. Mary's on Good Friday in 1400, were driven as much to escape the cold drizzle as to arrive on time for the service. Inside blazing torches cast dancing shadows on the stone floor and illuminated colourfully painted walls depicting various saints. Though the atmosphere was unusually solemn, everyone looked forward to the richly symbolic rituals that re-enacted the crucifixion.

Vicar John Peche stood to one side of the chancel with bowed head as a chaplain read the passion narrative from the Gospel of John. When he read the words, *They parted my garments among them*, two clerks dramatically parted and removed the linen cloths that had been carefully arranged on the otherwise bare altar.

Prayers followed the reading, and then as if on cue, people turned to watch as two priests carrying a large veiled crucifix entered through the great west doors. As they proceeded towards the chancel, Vicar Peche and his assistants sang a series of scripture verses contrasting God's goodness with the ingratitude of

His people. The cross was then unveiled and all invited to approach it.

Clergy and congregation alike removed their shoes. Getting down on their knees, they crept forward to kiss the foot of the cross. This act of adoration completed, people returned to their places for the final part of the service, the *Kiss of Peace*. A deacon held out an object known as a *pax*[11] and each person kissed it in turn.

No one left the church at the conclusion of the service, however, because one of the most powerful ceremonies of the year was about to begin: the burial of Christ in the Easter sepulchre.

The atmosphere was hushed as Vicar Peche exited the chancel by way of the Priest's door. Once in the vestry, he removed his alb, amice and shoes. While he was gone, the other priests began lighting candles before the sepulchre. By the time they had finished, Peche reappeared wearing his surplice. In each hand he carried an object wrapped in a linen cloth. One was a silver pyx[12] containing the consecrated host. The other was the *pax* people had kissed during the liturgy. He paused briefly before the nave and held out his bundles for parishioners to see. Then moving back to the north side of the chancel, he placed the shrouded objects in the sepulchre. Another priest stood by his side and intoned Psalm 88:4, *I am counted with those who go down to the pit*. The chaplain who had earlier read from the Gospel of John, swung a censor over the sepulchre, diffusing a steamy vapour of frankincense.

The ceremony was officially over, and everyone left except for the clerk, the sexton, and the sexton's brother-in-law who were appointed to keep vigil over the host until Easter morning. They kept the candles burning and guarded the valuable pyx in which the sacrament was "buried." In turn, the church provided meat and ale for the men during the watch.

Easter morning finally arrived and the congregation entered to find the church ablaze with candles and torches. The priests assembled and proceeded to the sepulchre where they once again censed the tomb. All eyes were glued on the Vicar as he solemnly removed the host from its linen wrapping and replaced it in the hanging pyx above the altar. Next he unwrapped the crucifix and raised it from the sepulchre. With the priests in procession behind him, he carried it triumphantly around the church while the clerks sang a hymn.

Throughout the week, the empty tomb remained the focus of the services. Candles burned continuously before the sepulchre and the priest censed it every evening before vespers. And so passed the first Easter of the new century.

Bread in Their Pockets

If the 1300's were terrible, the 1400's were fabulous by comparison. A new middle class was emerging, and prosperity and piety were on the rise. St. Mary's enjoyed the attention of a number of historical figures from this period whose imprints are still visible in the church today.

In spite of their piety, however, parishioners had grown slack in obeying a 250-year-old decree. In 1406, the Bishop of Lincoln issued a "polite notice" reminding St. Mary's parishioners not to neglect their annual trek to the martyr's tomb at St. Albans. The annual walk could be undertaken during the six days after Ascension Day or just before Whitsunday (Pentecost).

Today, that pilgrimage is re-enacted every year on Easter Monday. It is a voluntary act of celebration followed by an outdoor worship service on the lawns of the Abbey. Though predominantly geared to youth, people of all ages set out early from St. Mary's for the 10-mile journey to St. Albans. They are joined by thousands of others from the diocese, and the event is capped off by a procession past the martyr's shrine.

Like the pilgrimage, Holy Communion in the 15th century was also an annual event for parishioners, usually at Easter. While the clergy communicated weekly during the Mass, churchgoers had to be content with a sort of substitute ceremony every Sunday. Each week, a different household brought a loaf of bread to the service. Before the liturgy began, the person providing the bread took it to the High Altar, said a prayer and presented it to the priest for his blessing. Not everyone ate the bread at the end of the service, though. Some people carried it in their pocket throughout the week, believing it would ward off evil.

As it does today, a time of intercessory prayer occurred just prior to the offering. This portion of the service, known as the *bidding of the bedes*, was in English. The priest led from the pulpit, directing people to pray for those in authority: the Pope, bishops, clergy, their own priests, the King, the lords, and the mayor. They also prayed for the pregnant women of the parish, pilgrims, travellers, the sick, the family providing the holy loaf and the recently deceased.

The Chaplain's Expensive Gifts

Sometime before 6 March 1417, a chaplain named John Spitele died and was buried in the churchyard. Spitele left two significant items: his memorial brass, thought to be the oldest in the church, and a will, providing a picture of medieval life at St. Mary's. The document tells us that a large staff assisted the Vicar, Master John Blomham, including parish priests, stipendiary priests, a deacon, a parish clerk and a sacristan.[13]

In his will, John Spitele left the church:

> ...a new antiphonary scored by his own hand on condition that it is always placed in the north choir there and not with the Vicar on the south side at Mass and at the other hours of the day as long as it may last and if anyone does to the contrary, his exors are to take back the aforesaid antiphonary and take it with them out of the church without hindrance and freely give it to

the royal chapel of Westminster palace to be kept there fore ever...[14]

Aside from that unusual stipulation, he also bequeathed St. Mary's six service books written in his own hand; a gilt chalice depicting the annunciation of the Virgin Mary; a paten,[15] decorated *with a figure of Christ crowning his most blessed Mother*; a communion cloth to be used at the altar of the Chapel of St. Katherine; and vestments of silk cloth.

John Spitele

Like William Wenlock of the previous century, Spitele paid to have Masses sung for his soul. Additionally, he left 12d. for the sacristan *for ringing the bells and making his grave and for drink during the time of ringing*. He also requested that candles be burned around his body and that *the unused residue of the wax be used at private Masses outside the chancel*.

Spitele's memorial brass depicting his likeness was originally located in the floor of the chancel but now resides in the north wall of Wenlock Chapel. The brass figures represent John on the right (wearing priest's robes) and that of his parents. Unfortunately, the figure of his mother is missing.

Dangerous Books

Forty years after John Wycliffe's death, his influence still irked powerful clergymen. In 1422, Abbot Wheathamstead summoned St. Mary's Vicar, John Penthelyn, and other local priests to St. Albans to discuss the matter. Penthelyn, instituted at St. Mary's around 1418, held degrees in both canon and civil law.

Wheathamstead grilled the men about Wycliffe's influence in their parishes, charging them to keep a close watch on anyone suspected of following these teachings. He also asked the clergymen if they possessed *any* books in English. One of the priests confessed to not only reading one, but encouraging others to do so as well. Wheathamstead demanded the offensive book and had it burned. For penance the guilty priest had to make an annual barefoot pilgrimage to the Abbey and approach the martyr's tomb walking backwards.

Stone carving of Abbot Wheathamstead

The Abbot, keenly aware of his duty to discipline, gave equal attention to his obligations as St. Mary's patron. Though the church tower had been completed in the previous century, it apparently lacked bells until 1430. Records indicate that four were purchased that year, and parishioners solicited a contribution from Abbot Wheathamstead. That worthy man dutifully coughed up 100 shillings and promised to pay for the entire fourth bell out of his own pocket – on one condition: that God allow him to continue as Abbot for another seven years, which he did. The Abbot also saw to it that a considerable part of St. Mary's chancel was rebuilt before his death in 1465. The fourfold sedilia,[16] which bears his motto and heraldic arms, is attributed to him as well.

Speeding through Purgatory

John Spitele's brass may be the oldest in the church, but John Penthelyn was probably the first Vicar to have had such a memorial. In any case, his is the first of which there is any evidence. The brass bore his likeness, and a label protruding from his mouth contained the words: *Christi passis sit mihi salus sempiterna et protector* (The steps of Christ are to me safety and protection forever). All that remains now is this label inserted into the south wall of Wenlock Chapel, close to the chancel doorway where he was buried.

Penthelyn, probably a Welshman, died the 18th of February 1444. His will, translated from Latin, begins:

> In the Name of God, Amen. The 10th day of February 1444. I John Penthelyn, Vicar of Luyton, being of sound body and sane memory (having made) a beneficial premeditation of the day of my last journey, and considering the insecure state of this present life, and minding that the days of man on earth are short, and not wishing to leave my goods so accumulated undisposed of, to the glory and honour of our same Lord Jesus Christ, I ordain and dispose of my goods in this manner. First, I bequeathed my soul to Almighty God and the Blessed Mary, His mother, and my body to be buried with ecclesiastical rites….

Penthelyn directed that every priest attending his funeral and burial Mass receive 20d., every deacon 12d., and every clerk 10d. His will also mentions *spiritual sons* he sponsored for baptism; he provided each with a sheep. A further 12 shillings and 4d. was distributed among the poor. Two clergymen received his six clerical gowns and one of them his *Portiforia* – the breviary a priest carried with him when he travelled. Handwritten, it contained the daily services and prayers, along with musical notes. These books were expensive before the advent of printing and commonly bequeathed from one clergyman to another.

Penthelyn also provided for two priests – one in Luton and another in Wales – to say Masses daily for his soul for a year.

Obviously if one had the means to shorten a painful stay in purgatory, why risk leaving it to the good will and expense of others? This "prayer for hire" idea seemed to guarantee the wealthy a fast track to heaven. Contrary to the popular saying, it appeared that at least indirectly, some believed you *could* take it with you!

The Revd Robert Burgh succeeded Penthelyn and remained in Luton nine years before resigning in 1454. To replace Burgh, Abbot John de Wheathamstead appointed Master John Lammer to the post, where he stayed for 23 years.

John Hay of Stopsley, steward to the Archbishop of Canterbury and a man of considerable means, also left his mark on the church. He is credited with adding the clearstory and restoring the north aisle at his own expense. He was buried under that aisle in 1455. A brass memorial marked the spot, but unfortunately was destroyed by later renovations. What survives from the inscription has been placed in the wall next to the stairway in Wenlock Chapel.

John Hay

Laundering Ransom Money

One of St. Mary's best-known historical figures is Sir John Wenlock. A great nephew of the priest William Wenlock, Sir John was a wealthy knight under Henry VI. He served as Constable of Baneburgh Castle and Chamberlain to Queen Margaret. In 1461, after defecting to the Yorkist side, he accompanied Edward of York on his victorious entrance into London. Under Edward he became a Baron, Chief Butler of England, Steward of Berkhamstead Castle and Lieutenant of Calais. He also represented Bedfordshire in Parliament and was Speaker of the House of Commons.

By the year 1460, Wenlock owned nearly one-half of Luton Manor, among his other properties and estates. Lands and titles are transitory, however, and as a more lasting legacy he built the Wenlock Chapel. He intended it to be a memorial to his first wife Elizabeth, as well as a chantry[17] and family tomb.

A small hindrance existed to building the chapel, however: Wenlock did not own it. The rights to Someries Chapel, as it was called, were attached to Someries Manor. Fortunately it was only a question of money, which Wenlock possessed. He purchased the manor, and set about remaking and enlarging the chapel. To accommodate the new dimensions, the vestry had to migrate east a few feet until it extended a fraction beyond the end of the chancel. A casualty of the move was the chancel's north window that had overlooked the churchyard. Now it inconveniently looked into the vestry…which is why someone eventually plastered it over.

These trifling vexations aside, Sir John's contribution has been appreciated through the centuries. However, today people might be a little uncomfortable with the way he supposedly financed it…with ransom money! Ransoming captured soldiers was an acceptable practice of the day. And the nobility wore expensive armour, making them easy targets. Wenlock, who participated in several campaigns against the French, had ample opportunity for making such captures. Mr. Tavener of Harlington, an author writing in 1648 and related to the Lords of the Manor at Biscot, claimed that the Wenlock Chapel was built on the spoils of the French Wars. Regardless of where he got it, Wenlock possessed sufficient wealth to lend Henry VI £1,033 (around £360,000 in today's currency).

While knights built chapels with money from ransomed soldiers, Rome financed the Pope's building projects by selling indulgences. An indulgence shortened one's time in purgatory or brought exemptions from religious requirements imposed upon the general population. In fact, in January 1466 the ever-generous Lord Wenlock petitioned the Pope for an indulgence on behalf of St. Mary's. As a result, parishioners were permitted to eat milk products during Lent and at other fasts. He later petitioned the Pope on his own behalf. He wanted the Pontiff to direct parishioners to *pray for his good estate in life* and after his death to say a Pater Noster and an Ave for him (if laymen) and the Psalm *Miserere mei Deus* (if clergy).

Wenlock's Game Plan for Here and After

Lord Wenlock was aiming to be paroled from purgatory at the earliest possible date and counting on his money to help. As a warrior, the burden of blood sullied his hands and conscience. Aside from Wenlock's own chantry at St. Mary's, his second wife provided another. A third was in existence as far back as 1462 when a London clothier's widow endowed a chantry in St. Christopher's, on behalf of Lord Wenlock, King Edward IV and his father Richard of York.

Wenlock was a first-team player in the War of the Roses, for *both* sides. No one knows exactly why he changed loyalties several times, perhaps partly because defeat meant losing lands, titles, power and wealth.

Wenlock met his end at the Battle of Tewkesbury in 1471, fighting for the Lancastrians. He was supposedly buried in the nearby Abbey. At one time there was a depiction of Wenlock in the east window of his chapel, with the following inscription:

> Jesu Christ, most of myght,
> have mercy on John le Wenlock, Knight,
> and of his wiffe Elizabeth,
> Wch owt of this world is past by death.

> Wch ffounded this chapell here.
> Helpe them with your hearty prair.
> That they may come to that place
> Where ever is joy and solace.

Wenlock's death was untimely. It occurred while his allegiance was on the wrong side of the crown. Thus Edward IV granted his lands to Thomas Rotherham, the Bishop of Lincoln who eventually became Archbishop of York. Rotherham must have been quite the politician as well; he had appointments as Lord Chancellor and Ambassador to France. Even the Pope was impressed, and elevated him to Cardinal in 1480.

A Noble Club for the Middle Class

In between the years he served in government, Rotherham founded a religious guild in Luton, *The Guild of the Holy and Undivided Trinity and of the Blessed Virgin Mary*. The License, dated 12 May 1472, bore the signature of King Edward IV and listed twelve other founding members including the Archbishop's brother, John Rotherham, their mother Alice, John Acworth, and John Lammer the Vicar.

Licenses for religious guilds were provided for a fee and with the understanding that members would pray for the King's soul and the souls of his family. Nor was the fee a trifling sum. The King's coffers gained £72 in the transaction.

Vicar John Lammer

An illustration in the Guild's lavishly illuminated register depicts the Archbishop, the King and Queen and the founders, including St. Mary's Vicar, John Lammer.

Archbishop Rotherham, founder of the Guild of the Holy Trinity.

Painting from the Guild Register. Archbishop Rotherham is kneeling in front, while Vicar John Lammer is the third figure to his left.

A lavishly illuminated page from the Guild's Register.

One could be excused for mistaking the Guild of the Holy Trinity for an exclusive club. In its first year, the rolls included Sir Godfrey Boleyn, Lord Mayor of London (and great grandfather of Anne Boleyn), Lord Hoo and Hastings, and Edmund Grey Earl of Kent. Interesting enough, two members were enrolled posthumously: Sir John Wenlock and John Hay. Even if you were dead, membership had its benefits in the form of ongoing prayer for your soul!

Religious guilds or fraternities were popular in the Middle Ages and Bedfordshire had at least seventeen. These Guilds enabled the middle class to have what only the rich could previously afford: a priest to say Masses for their souls. So in this sense, the Guild of the Holy Trinity was definitely not a posh club only for the nobility. Of course, the wealthy were not excluded from the Guild because their contributions were welcome also. Luton's landowners of that period were all members of the fraternity. Apparently dues were not required, but members made donations and bequests in their wills.

The Guild of the Holy Trinity established a chapel and altar in St. Mary's – probably next to the Hoo Chapel or in the south transept – and paid two chaplains to minister there.

The Annual "Tea"

Generally speaking, all guilds existed to promote brotherly love, charity and social events. Specific goals of the Guild of the Holy Trinity were to maintain a school, provide relief to the poor and hold an annual procession and feast. How long the fraternity held to its lofty purposes is not clear, but the account book for its final five years reveals that no money went to support either a school or the poor. Social aims were not neglected, however, as records for the annual feasts testify. These celebrations were held over a weekend towards the end of May and frequently cost more than £20, almost seven thousand pounds by today's valuation.

Existing accounts from one year show that this grand medieval feast featured 82 geese, 47 pigs, 65 capons, 74 chickens, 84 rabbits and 20 lambs as well as beef and salmon. The absence of peacock and swan on the menu hints that Royal guests were not in attendance. Much of the meat probably went into a kind of stew known as *mortress*. It consisted of boiled chicken and pork mixed with grated bread, broth, egg yolks and hot spices.

Preparation for the feast began days in advance, and members of the Guild or relatives supplied, cooked and serviced the event. Because the meat had to be acquired early, a hired man watched and made sure it did not spoil. The taste of meat at the point of putrefying, however, could be masked with a heavy dose of spices! Medieval feasts were as impressive for their size and expense, as they were for their lack of sanitation, compared to today's standards.

The extravaganza also included entertainment, but records only give the tiniest glimpse, noting that *Thomas Thredder accompanied on the harp*.

Guild members were referred to collectively as the *brothersed*. They met in the Brothersed House, located on the corner of Castle Street and Market Hill. A deed from the 17th century identifies this with the old Red Lion Inn, called *The Lion*.

At the Guild's dissolution in 1547, one source noted that the priests hired by the Fraternity were but *meanly lerned*, suggesting that they may not have been proficient in Latin.

For local historians, the Guild's Register is a significant document because it provides a record of many Luton families as far back as 1474. In contrast, St. Mary's earliest surviving Parish Register dates from 1603.

Luton's First Hole in the Wall

St. Mary's gained a new Vicar in 1477, Richard Barnard, who became Master of the Guild in the following year. Today Barnard is best known for the small but exquisite chantry that bears his name on the south side of the chancel. A rebus carved into the spandrels of the arches depicts a muzzled bear and angels holding boxes of 'nard' or spikenard. Together these pictures form the name Bar-nard. The chantry may have originally contained the stone effigy now found in a niche in the church's south wall. Some sources believe that it represents Barnard.

This chantry is truly one of the architectural gems of St. Mary's, but its purpose remains a mystery. Some have suggested it served as a leper chapel, allowing the afflicted to observe services from the outside through an open window. Others maintain it was a reliquary[18] or a confessional. It may have also been where the Blessed Sacrament was reserved for the sick and dying.

The chantry also featured an early "hole in the wall" prototype! People deposited their offerings through a slot in the outer buttress; from there the money slid into a recess. By moving a small sill slab on the inside, the stone back turned and a priest could retrieve the offerings.[19] Unfortunately, the device was covered over during the restoration of the small chapel in the early part of the 20th century.

In 1490, Lady Alice Rotherham died and was buried in Wenlock chapel. Her son, the Archbishop, supposedly provided her large altar tomb covered with a memorial brass. A depiction of Lady Rotherham carved into the brass shows her wearing the garments of a widow.

When the Rotherhams came into possession of Someries Manor after Sir John Wenlock's death, they also acquired the rights to the chapel. Sir John Rotherham (brother of the Archbishop) passed away in 1492. His will stated that his body was to be *buried before the image of St. Thomas a Becket the martyr, in my chapel annexed to the Church of Luton on the north side.*

His tomb and that of his wife are located against the north wall near the east end of the chapel. The tomb is canopied and would have contained brass figures at one time.

A Murder Plot

The year that John Rotherham died also saw the passing of Vicar Barnard. Thomas Ramridge of Luton, the Abbot of St. Albans, selected Adrian Castello as the next Vicar of St. Mary's. A foreigner from Italy, Castello's appointment was unusual. Italians were chosen to fill wealthy ecclesiastical posts in England, but this was the only time one was appointed to St. Mary's.

Although Adrian de Castello came from humble origins, a benefactor paid for his education. Castello's knowledge and merit propelled him up the clerical ladder and attracted the attention of Pope Innocent VIII. The Pontiff sent him to England where he received a number of preferments, indicating his popularity with the religious establishment. A curate performed Castello's duties at St. Mary's, since he was also prebend of St. Paul's Cathedral and held the Rectory of St. Dunstan during the same period.

While still officially St. Mary's Vicar, Castello returned to Rome to serve as the King's representative. Not until he became Bishop of Hereford in 1502, did he have to relinquish his position at Luton.

For all his achievements and honours, Adrian de Castello found a not-so-honourable place in St. Mary's history when he conspired to murder Pope Leo X in the next century.

Before committing himself to the plot, Castello visited a well-known astrologer in the Appennines. He tested the woman with a copy of his own horoscope, asking about the person to whom it belonged.

"If it is a man," replied the astrologer, "then he would be a cardinal."

Bingo! Castello was a cardinal! Encouraged, he ventured to ask how long the Pope would live and who would succeed him.

"The Pope will not live much longer and his successor will be a man of humble origins named Adrian, who owing to his own virtue alone, deserves the honour," the astrologer predicted.[20]

As the only member of the College of Cardinals with that name and based on some other details given by the woman, Castello concluded he was to be the next Pope. This was the catalyst that launched him down the road of destruction. The plot was discovered and he and his co-conspirators arrested.

At the trial, Castello was judged guilty beyond all question, fined, deprived of his honours and exiled from Rome. A few years later, around 1526, he died in the obscurity into which he was born.

In the next century, another clergyman would also live to regret consulting an astrologer.

6.
English is Hot, Purgatory's Not

The wrenchings of divorce rocked St. Mary's following the break-up between His Holiness and His Highness in the 1500's. Whether the split was a triumph or a tragedy depended on which side of the theological fence you stood. St. Mary's had Vicars from both sides.

The new century began calmly enough for the church, with Archbishop Rotherham marking the occasion by presenting to St. Mary's a gilt chalice and two cruets. Adrian de Castello was still Luton's Vicar in absentia. His elevation to the bishopric two years later opened the door for St. Albans' Abbot to appoint the next Vicar. However, the King's mother, Margaret, Countess of Richmond, asked the Abbot to pass the honour to the Speaker of the House of Commons, Sir Robert Sheffield. Who could refuse the King's mother? As it turned out, the Speaker had a relative in mind for the position, Edward Sheffield, LL.D. Sheffield was instituted on 9 May 1502 and held the living for 24 years.

During his tenure at St. Mary's, Sheffield also held appointments as Canon of Lichfield, Rector of Cambourne in Cornwall, and Rector of Yatt in Gloucestershire. He chose to live and minister in Luton, however, so others carried out his duties elsewhere.

Sheffield's large brass memorial located in the floor of the south transept depicts him wearing processional vestments and the cap of a Doctor of Divinity. He is elevating the host, but the wafer has been scratched out, perhaps by zealous Reformers. Sheffield had his brass engraved and placed in the chancel before his death. Though the date of his decease was never filled in on the memorial, he obviously died sometime between the date of his will (17 Dec. 1525) and its probate (7 Feb. 1526).

Priest Edward Sheffield served as St. Mary's Vicar for 24 years.

A couple of years into Sheffield's incumbency, yet another Rotherham went to his resting place in the Wenlock Chapel. Sir Thomas Rotheram, a nephew of the Archbishop of York, died in 1504. Unfortunately his memorial brass no longer exists.

Looking After the Saints

A church the size of St. Mary's required a great deal of wax, and not merely to light the interior on dark days. Candles had to be kept burning before all the images of the saints. People commonly bequeathed money for this expense.

52

John Dermer, a former warden of the Guild of the Holy Trinity, was very conscientious in this respect. His will (1504) gave 2d. each to the lights of the Holy Cross in the rood loft, the Holy Cross, 'le grene rode,' St. Mary of Pity, and St. John the Baptist. But to St. Katherine, St. Margaret, St. Sithe, St. George and St. Clement, Mr. Dermer left 5d. each for lights, an indication that these were the saints he especially applied to for help.

What appears to be an ingenious method of tithing popped up during this period. *Forgotten tithes* as they were called, were bequests to the church covering the amount a person may have inadvertently overlooked during his lifetime.

For instance, in 1509 John Barber left 3s. 4d. to the high altar of St. Mary's for forgotten tithes. It seems a clever way of giving God His due *after* you no longer needed it! But actually they were a kind of insurance against having to stay in purgatory a moment longer than absolutely necessary.

The nature of these bequests show the importance parishioners placed on tithing. Regardless of their motivation, they gave it scrupulous attention.

John Barber was the son of John and Agnes Barber, whose partial memorial brass can still be seen on the floor of the North Transept.[21] Aside from the forgotten tithes, his will also provided £3 6s. 8d. for his burial near his father in the transept, just below the west wall.

Sixteen years separates John Barber's will from Edward Sheffield's but during that time an interesting change took place. Barber's will was written in the customary Latin while Sheffield's was in English.

Several other wealthy men of the period also bequeathed gifts to St. Mary's. Thomas Crawley, another member of the Guild of the Holy Trinity, died in 1511 and left 20d. for *tythes forgotten*, a silver candlestick, an antiphoner and £2 for church repairs. His will also directed his body to be buried before the altar of the Holy Trinity.

Knights in Shining Brass

One of the purposes of having a large brass memorial was to solicit the prayers of those who walked by and noticed it.

A founding member of the Guild, John Acworth, boasts a splendid brass. He is depicted in full armour between his wives, Alys and Amy. Below are seventeen figures representing the original eight brothers and nine sisters of the Guild. The Acworths were landed gentry, and John was the Lord of the manor of Biscot. At one time, St. Mary's contained several Acworth brasses, but only this one has survived.

Sir John Acworth

Among the largest and best preserved in the church, is the brass of John Sylam and his two wives. He died in 1513 and left St. Mary's seven pounds towards the purchase of a silver candlestick, three pounds for repairs to the church, £32 to pay for Masses for himself and his friends over the next 10 years, and £26 13s. for funeral expenses. Enough for an impressive ceremony! Sylam's marble tombstone with inlaid brass shows him in knight's armour standing between his wives, Elizabeth and Joan. The inscription exhorts:

Lady Acworth, a pious model of 15th century fashion

Off yo charite pray for the sowllis of John Sylam Elizabeth and Jone his wives the whych John decesyd

the x day of Juin in the yere of owre Lord mccccc and
xiii on whose sowllis Jh'u have m'cy. Amen.

Two parish priests – John Aleyn and Robert Wright – were witnesses to several wills during the early part of the century. They probably officiated alongside the Vicar, Dr. Sheffield, since three priests were needed for a full service.

Cardinal Wolsey's Durable Door

By the time Sheffield died, Cardinal Wolsey had already been appointed by Henry VIII to take charge of St. Albans Abbey. While acting as St. Mary's patron, Cardinal Wolsey presented the church with an impressive wooden door. A door may not sound like a great gift, but 450 years later it's still in use!

Wolsey also presented St. Mary's with their next Vicar, Richard Doke, who also held a doctorate. Doke was a Fellow of Exeter College, Oxford, as well as Vice-chancellor of the University in 1519. His appointment as Archdeacon of Salisbury the same year he came to St. Mary's may be the reason he resigned his role at Luton.

Thomas Herytage, who succeeded Doke as Vicar of St. Mary's, knew his predecessor while they were both at Oxford. Herytage was the Vicar when Thomas Cromwell ordered every church to have an English Bible on display. Times had changed since Abbot Wheathamstead opposed *any* book in English, much less the Bible.

Due to their expensive nature, these Bibles were chained down to prevent theft. The cost of St. Mary's first English Bible – as well as the lectern to which it was chained, was evenly divided between the congregation and the Vicar.

Cromwell introduced other changes also, one of which brought about St. Mary's first parish registers. He ordered the registration of all baptisms, marriages and deaths, and that each be taxed.

Although the amount was comparatively small, it worked a further hardship on the poorer families of the Parish.

A local law passed in 1528 reveals one of the social concerns of the day: top spinning. The court ruled that adults of the parish should cease playing at top spinning and devote their free time to learning. Top spinning was punishable by a 24-hour stay in the stocks, which happened to be located in the north corner of St. Mary's churchyard.

During the years that Herytage officiated at St. Mary's, Henry VIII severed Rome's authority from the English Church so that he could divorce Catherine and marry Ann Boleyn. What the Vicar thought of these acts is not recorded. Some clergy regretted the changes, while others, having been influenced by the reformers on the Continent, welcomed them.

Herytage's will, written in October 1537, indicated that he died with unpaid debts:

> I Thomas Herytage make my will and testament in the manner following: first I bequeath bothe my soule and body to be at the pleasure of the Holy Trinitie, and my goodes to be distributed to suche as I owe money unto and other wages charitable. I wolde also as litill cost as may be doon honestly on my buriall unto my detts be paid.

Composer of Songs and Strife

When Herytage passed away in 1537, a musically talented Welshman, John Gwynneth, succeeded him. Passionate and pugilistic, particularly when it came to the Catholic faith, Gwynneth was also a musician and the earliest known author among St. Mary's Vicars.

Like Adrian de Castello, he was of modest beginnings but showed great promise early in life. A mentor predicted Gwynneth would become a champion of Catholicism by writing against the

*The bass part from My Love Mourneth by John Gwynneth.
This hymn, preserved in the British Library, is the only one
that survives of all his musical compositions.*

heretics, as Protestants were known. Music captured his heart, however; he pursued a doctorate in that field after he became a priest. In applying for his degree, Gwynneth noted that he had written *all the responses of the whole year in division song, and had published three Masses of five parts and five Masses of four, and also certain symphonies, antiphonas and divers songs for the use of the church.*[22]

One of his hymns, "My Love Mourneth," was printed in 1530 in *A Boke of Twenty Songes Set to Music.*[23] Unfortunately, in those early days of music publishing, the different parts of a song were printed in separate books. The only existing copy of *Twenty Songes* contains bass parts so the melody is lost. A sweetness in his lyrics (see Appendix A), however, helps offset a less savoury impression Gwynneth gives from his books and court battles.

Disputing Heretics

The year before his appointment as Vicar, Gwynneth fulfilled his mentor's prediction when he took up his pen against the late John Frith, a reformer burnt at the stake three years previously. Frith's writings against transubstantiation[24] and purgatory continued to circulate, and Gwynneth considered them an insidious threat to Catholicism. After his institution at St. Mary's, he published two more volumes attacking Frith's book. Printing was still relatively new, but both Catholic and Protestant Christians were quick to make use of the new invention.

Technology for printing may have been available, but writing styles still needed refining. For instance, John Gwynneth's titles are nothing more than lengthy run-on sentences describing their contents. The books that still survive (in the spelling of the day) are:

1. *The confutations of the fyrst parte of Frythes boke, with a disputacyon before, whether it be possible for any heretike to know that hymselfe is one or not…..*(1536)

2. *A declaration of the state, wherein all heretikes dooe lead their lives: and also of their continuall indever and propre fruites…..(1554)*

3. *A manifest detection of the notable falshed of that part of John Frithe's boke, which he calleth his foundacion, and bosteth it to be invincible….(1554)*

4. *A playne demonstration of J. Frithes lack of witte and learnynge in his understandynge of holie Scripture….(1557)*

All of his books take the form of a dialogue between two characters: Catholicus and Hereticus. His explanations are often difficult to follow and his tone sometimes condescending.

Shortly after arriving at St. Mary's, Gwynneth began work on his second book attacking Frith and his beliefs. Curious to see how it would look in print, he sent off the first several chapters to be published as an essay. But before finishing the manuscript, Gwynneth fell ill. While the Vicar was in London for treatment, the printer managed to acquire his entire draft and proceeded to edit it into a book for Gwynneth's approval.

When the Vicar found out, he was furious and refused to allow it to be published, later explaining, *not only because he did so much without my consent, but also specially because it was done before I had perused and duly examined that I had written.*[25]

Gwynneth felt the printer had taken liberties because he needed the work. Disgusted with the whole matter, he stopped writing. Seventeen years later he picked up the pen again, explaining that although he had not intended to write any further after the fiasco with the printer,

> little thinking then, that the venom of Frith's book would have spread so far abroad, as the lamentable experience thereof does presently declare…I have returned unto my first purpose again, and so gone

> forward with all that I have newly written…with such alteration thereof, as the time and change of things has since ministered great and worthy of occasion.[26]

It might be unfair to conclude that Gwennyth was obsessed with John Frith, but it would not be far off the mark to say that the Welshman had a vindictive streak. This is evident from a dispute the Vicar pursued in the courts long after it had been resolved in his favour.

It began when Henry VIII presented him to the provostship of Clynog Vaur in the Diocese of Bangor. But Bishop Capon, who held the patronage by right, refused to admit Gwynneth and instead instituted a man of his own choosing, Gregory Williamson.

Gwynneth was not about to be deprived and pursued the matter in the courts. When Bishop Capon moved to Salisbury, Gwynneth took legal action against his successor, Bishop Bird. This Bishop was shortly removed to Chester, and Gwynneth was finally instituted to Clynog by the commissary of Archbishop Cranmer.

But Gwynneth refused to let the matter die. He obtained summonses against Bishop Bird and Bishop Capon, as well as Gregory Williamson. Because the Bishops had moved to other places, they could not appear and Gwynneth won the judgement by default. Once again, the matter should have ended, but St. Mary's Vicar continued his pugilistic course, fighting a two-year legal battle with Bishop Bird's replacement.

An End to the Relationship

The dissolution of St. Alban's in 1539 meant that the income St. Mary's had sent the Abbey for nearly 400 years now flowed to Henry's coffers. Unaffected financially by the change, Gwynneth continued to receive the vicarial tithes and other usual dues through the reigns of the reforming Edward VI and the Roman Catholic Mary.

Religious reforms did affect the number of officiating priests at St. Mary's, however. Between the years 1545 and 1547, the church had approximately 1200 communicants, but records indicate that Gwynneth may have been the sole minister during his last 10 years as Vicar.

Gwynneth remained silent when changes were forced upon the church. Although he did not publish so much as a tract, one can imagine him grinding his teeth at each new decree. In 1547 the order came to remove images from the churches. If the Parish complied, the image of the Virgin Mary over the main altar and the large crucifix suspended from the chancel arch would have come down. Some believe that Gwynneth hid these rather than having them destroyed.

Selling Off the Silver

The year 1547 also saw the demise of the Guild of the Holy Trinity. An Act of Parliament granted Henry VIII the property of all chantries, hospitals and guilds, but the King died before the property could be confiscated. However, the grant was renewed to Edward VI who seized the Guild and St. Mary's chantries for the crown. Gwynneth was the last Vicar to hold membership in the Guild.

Because Edward had taken over the wealth of the guilds and chantries, churchwardens probably feared he would also confiscate valuable ornaments no longer permitted in the liturgy. Rather than be robbed of their value, many churches sold these items and used the money for renovations. This may have been the case at St. Mary's when the parish approved the churchwardens Edward Crawley and John Punter to sell

-a paxe of silver with a pece of mother of perle
-a pixe of silver and gylte with a doble glass

-ij challeesess with their pattents doble gylte

The items yielded £15, equivalent to about £1900 today, and the money was spent on repairing one of the aisles.

Several momentous changes rocked the church in 1549, including the change from a Latin to English liturgy. Clergy were also granted the right to marry, and an Act of Uniformity enforced the use of a new English prayer book.

Gwynneth must have been ecstatic when the Catholic Queen Mary came to power in 1553. Three days after she ascended the throne, he preached a sermon entitled *The Declaration of the Notable Victory given of God to Queen Mary*. The sermon was printed but no copy survives today.

With Mary on the throne, Gwynneth plunged back into his fight against heretics and produced two more books attacking Frith and Protestantism.

Meanwhile, Queen Mary permitted the return of images and large crucifixes in the churches. She also reinstated the services commonly used in the last years of Henry VIII. But the three years England's Church was reconciled to Rome was a brutal time for many Protestants, including a future Vicar of St. Mary's.

Paying Back the Church

While on the throne, Queen Mary had a team of commissioners investigating churches which had sold their sacred implements during King Edward's reign. St. Mary's did not escape their scrutiny. Since former churchwarden Edward Crawley had died, his executor, John Crawley, had to explain why the *pax*, pyx and chalices were sold and how the money was spent.

His explanation failed to satisfy the commissioners, however. They ruled that Crawley be responsible for seeing St. Mary's repaid the equivalent of £15 in church ornaments. Crawley raised most of the money from the congregation and made up the difference from his own pocket.

Gwynneth wrote to the commissioners that the task was completed according to their instructions:

> To the Worshipfull William Barners, Thomas Mildmaye and John Wyseman Esquyres, the Kynges and Quenes maiestes commissioners.
> This bill made the xth day of June in the second and third yeres of the reignes of our Sovereigne lord and ladye King Phillipp and Quene Mary us to certefye your worshipps that for the accomplishment of the order taken with John Crawley one of the executors of Edwarde Crawley sometyme churchewardeyn of the parishe Church of Luton in the countye of Bedford for the bestowing of jvli iijs iiijd uppon some necessary ornamentes for the saide churche. There is bestowed by the saide Crawley uppon a cope and a vestment of blew velvet with that belongeth unto them five poundes. There is also layed oute and bestowed uppon a chalys twenty nobles[27] and odd money. And this is doon at the charge of the saide Crawley.
> Per me Johannem Gwyneth, icarium ibidem[28]

The Vicar did not have long to enjoy his vestment of *blew velvett*, however. The Protestant Elizabeth ascended the throne in 1558, and the religious climate changed once again. Now the Catholics were persecuted and martyred. Gwynneth either resigned shortly afterwards or died while still Vicar.[29] In any case, Queen Elizabeth chose George Mason as St. Mary's next incumbent. Though instituted on 1 December 1558, it is unlikely Mason resided in Luton because he also held three other livings near London and was Prebend of St. Paul's as well as a Canon of Windsor. Undoubtedly his duties at St. Mary's fell to a curate.

The Vicar in Stocks and Bonds
When the Revd Mason died in 1562, Queen Elizabeth appointed Thomas Rose to the living at St. Mary's. A reformer, Rose preached vigorously against purgatory and praying to saints and images. He also had the distinction of appearing in an early edition of Foxe's Book of Martyrs.[30] To understand why he merited those pages, it's necessary to return to the reign of Henry VIII and the year 1529, when Rose had just been appointed to Hadleigh in Suffolk after completing his curacy.

About this time, crowds began flocking to a church in Essex to see a large crucifix associated with miracles. Apparently one of Rose's more effective sermons against worshipping images inspired four young men to steal the crucifix and set it afire. Rose had urged no such thing, however.

The men were apprehended, and three of them were found guilty of sacrilege and felony, and sentenced to death. Before going to the gallows they were offered their lives in exchange for implicating Rose, but they refused and were executed. Rose's adversaries still accused him of participating in the deed, and had him arrested and imprisoned at the Bishop of Lincoln's house in Holborn. He was placed in the stocks from Shrovetide (the three days that immediately precede Ash Wednesday) until 21 June 1533.

The Book of Martyrs records:

> The stocks were very high and great, so that day and night he did lie with his back on the ground, upon a little straw, with his heels so high, that by means the blood was fallen from his feet, which were almost without sense for a long time; and he herewith waxed very sick, insomuch that his keeper, pitying his estate, and hearing him cry sometimes, through the extremity of pain, went to the Bishop and told him that he would not keep him to die under his hand; and upon this he had some more ease and liberty.

Rose's supporters attempted to visit him but had no success until they bribed his keeper with four shillings. Even at that, they could only talk to Rose through a grate.

In midsummer, the prisoner was moved to Lambeth, where Archbishop Cranmer treated him courteously and eventually freed him with the provision that he stay at least 20 miles away from Hadleigh. Instead, Rose settled in London where he preached for six months. Supporters from Hadleigh eventually found him and begged him to return to their town. But Rose was unwilling to break his word to Cranmer. A knight by the name of Sir John Rainsford, however, intervened with the Archbishop on Rose's behalf, and Cranmer relented.

Rose returned to Hadleigh to find his previous position filled, so for the next three years he ministered in the nearby town of Stratford. His enemies, infuriated at his effective sermons, prevailed upon the Bishop of Norwich to forbid Rose to preach. Once again his supporters rallied around him and sent a signed petition to the Archbishop testifying to his character and honesty. Rose in the meantime fled to London and appealed to Lord Audley, a Chancellor favourably inclined toward reformers. Audley sent Rose to Thomas Cromwell with a recommendation that he be given a license from the King to preach. Cromwell did more than obtain a license for Rose; he made him his chaplain.

Secure for the time being, Rose continued preaching against auricular confession and transubstantiation, even though this violated the law and was punishable by death. Once Rose was out from under the protection of Cromwell, however, a number of men complained so vehemently to the Duke of Norfolk, that the Duke himself set out after him. He declared that whoever found Rose should hang him on the first available tree. Friends managed to warn Rose of the danger, and he left immediately for the Continent and company of other reformers in Zurich and Basle.

Kidnapped by Pirates

Rose attempted to return to England a little later, but discovered the climate was still dangerous and just barely succeeded in escaping back to Europe. Three years passed before he made another attempt to return, this time with his wife and his two-year-old child. When a storm disabled their ship, pirates overtook them and not only robbed the family of £40, but also held them for ransom.

Having no idea how long their imprisonment might last, Rose and his wife grew depressed. Divine Providence intervened four weeks later when a young man arrived to ransom several other British prisoners. He was surprised to find Rose, whom he had once heard preach. Fortunately the young man had been favourably impressed by the preacher, and he gladly paid for the family's freedom.

On returning to England, Rose kept a low profile in London for a year, until the death of Henry VIII in 1547. Five years later he received the position of Vicar of West Ham. It is interesting to note that Archbishop Cranmer recommended Thomas Rose to the King for consideration of the archbishopric of Armagh, the highest position in the Irish Church. Although Rose did not get the appointment, the recommendation tells us that Cranmer esteemed him highly.

A Treasonous Prayer

Unfortunately for Rose, King Edward's reign was cut short by his death. While St. Mary's Vicar John Gwynneth celebrated the return of a Catholic monarch to the throne, Rose lost his living and had to go into hiding. As in the past, friends came to his aid, made him their teacher and supported him with donations. He managed to avoid arrest for a year, until New Year's Day 1555. He was at a house meeting with 30 others when troops broke in and arrested them for petitioning God to *turn the heart of Queen Mary from idolatry or else shorten her days.* This of course, was considered treasonous.

Some sources claim that Rose was imprisoned in the tower of London only to escape, but this appears to be pure fiction. Possibly he was initially held at the tower, but Foxe claims he was taken to the Bishop of Winchester, who put him in his prison. Foxe dedicated nine pages to Rose in the *Book of Martyrs*, including his examinations before the Bishop.

When the Bishop was about to depart on a visit around his diocese, he committed Rose into the keeping of a knight, Sir William Woodhouse. The knight told the Bishop that he would provide *meat and drink and lodging* for the prisoner.

Escape

Aside from the basics, Woodhouse also gave the preacher a measure of liberty and then departed for two weeks. Rose heard a rumour that should he escape, Sir William would forfeit his life and lands. On his return, Rose asked him if it were true and Woodhouse denied it. Rose himself later wrote:

> Then I said, 'Sir, but for the reverence I bear you, I might have been a hundred miles from you ere this. But I trust now, sir, seeing you be not bound for me, I may go visit my friends.' 'Go where you will,' said Sir William; 'for' quoth he, 'I told the Bishop I would not be your jailer, but promised only meat, drink and lodging for you.'

Thus encouraged, Rose escaped. The Bishop was highly displeased when he returned to discover Rose missing and instituted a search, which proved fruitless. Frustrated, the Bishop resorted to a conjuror who told him that Rose had escaped over the water and was being hidden by a woman. The Bishop interpreted this to mean that Rose had fled overseas, so he abandoned the search.

Rose later found out about this and seemed amused.

> In very deed, I was passed over a small water and was hid by a blessed and godly woman, which lived in a poor cottage, the space of three weeks till all the great heat was over.

With the search called off, Rose travelled back to the Continent where he stayed until Queen Mary died in 1558. When he finally returned to England, Queen Elizabeth restored him to the living at West Ham, and six years later he became the Vicar of St. Mary's.

Aside from the distinction afforded him by Foxe, Rose also had the honour of being the first married priest at St. Mary's since Parliament passed the legislation in 1549.

Thomas Rose resigned in 1575, and William Horne, M.A. became the next Vicar in Luton. Horne, like Gwynneth, was also an author. He wrote a simple catechism published around 1580, explaining the basics of Christianity. Written in a question and answer format, it leaves no doubt that Horne believed in the reformation of the Church. To the question, *The bread then is not Christ's body?* he responds:

> No, for bodily the heavens holde him til the day of the resurrection of all thinges, but it represents his body, as the wine doth his blood, shewing, that by one oblation he hath consecrated for ever them that are sanctified.[31]

A copy of Horne's book survives today in the British Library.

In 1578, Richard Crawley, nephew of the aforementioned churchwarden, passed away and his will directed he be buried in Luton's Church, *so nighe my father as may conveniently be*. Richard had been a member of the Guild of the Holy Trinity, as had a number of his ancestors going back to the year 1479. His grandfather

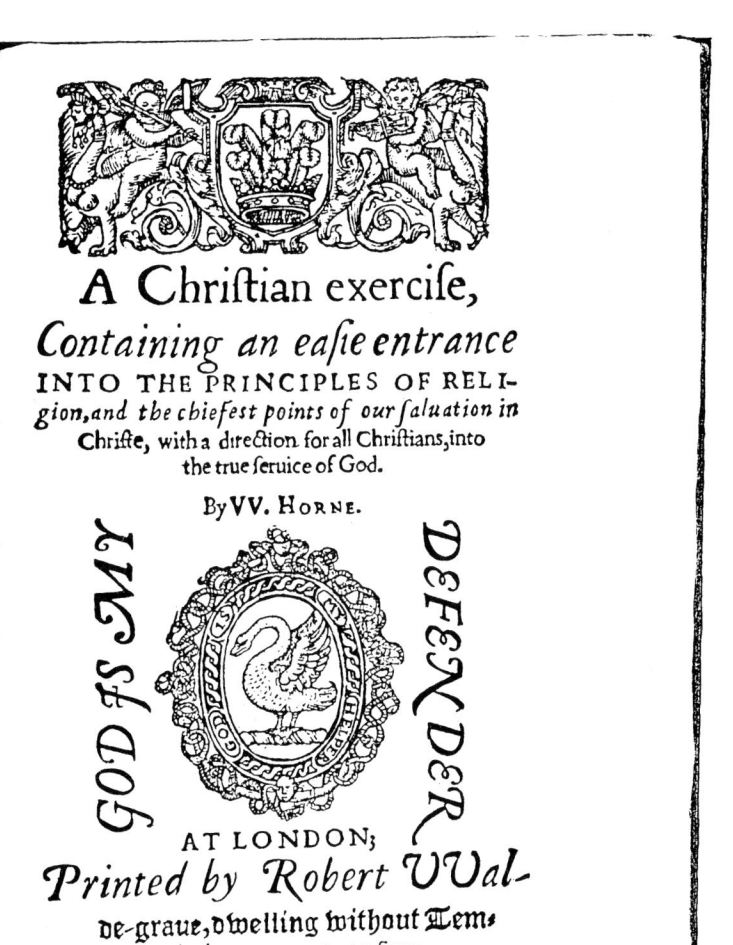

A Chriſtian exerciſe,
Containing an eaſie entrance
INTO THE PRINCIPLES OF RELI-
gion, *and the chiefest points of our ſaluation in*
Chriſte, *with a direction for all Chriſtians, into*
the true ſeruice of God.

By VV. HORNE.

GOD IS MY DEFENDER

AT LONDON;
Printed by Robert VVal-
de-graue, dwelling without Temple-barre, neere vnto Som-
merſet-houſe.

The title page to Vicar William Horne's book, A Christian Exercise, *published around 1580.*

Thomas Crawley had been Master of the Guild in 1502, and his Great-Grandfather William the warden in 1490.

A Plague of Indifference

During William Horne's incumbency, a new law stipulated that citizens had to attend their parish church at least once a month. Attendance throughout the country must have been falling or it may have been a scheme to force Catholics to hear Protestant teaching. In any case, the changing back and forth between Protestant and Catholic monarchs had resulted in a growing indifference among many of the laity. Regardless which doctrine a person believed, he alternately took on the label of either heretic or idolater…it just depended on who was in power.

If some parishioners were confused over doctrine, the congregation at St. Mary's was confused over who was now responsible for her repairs. While St. Albans possessed the great tithes, the Abbot was obliged to maintain the chancel. But responsibility for some of these practical details seemingly dissolved with the monasteries, and Luton's church suffered the resulting neglect.

Around 1586, a man named Camden passed through town. Regarding his visit to Luton he noted, "I saw nothing memorable, unless I should say that I saw a fair church, but the choir there was roofless and overgrown with weeds."

Horne died in Luton in 1594 and was buried in the chancel, which was beginning to resemble the churchyard. His tombstone contained the name Edith, indicating that he, too, was married.

Queen Elizabeth presented Edmund Brockett, M.A. to St. Mary's upon Horne's death. Brockett was probably a relative of the owner of Luton Hoo at that time, Sir John Brockett. This Vicar was married and had nine children, all of whom were baptised in the church.

St. Mary's had survived the turbulent 1500's, but her building bore evidence of the turmoil. The extent of the unseen spiritual damage she suffered would only become clear in the next century.

7.
St. Mary's Sun Roof

What was it like to attend St. Mary's when the choir was overgrown with weeds? Did the labourer cutting grass in the churchyard trim the weeds on the inside as well? How did people react during a Sunday Service when rain poured through the roofless chancel?

Was it rain or shame that finally drove the people to do something about the problem?

Perhaps both. In 1602, Churchwardens William Howe and Robert Barber sued the President of Trinity College, Oxford and George Wingate of Biscot over their obligation to repair the roofless chancel. Wingate and the President admitted to owning the rectorial tithes but argued that the freehold of the chancel remained in the Queen's hands, meaning she should repair it.

The court disagreed and ruled in favour of St. Mary's, ordering Oxford and Wingate to pay for repairs. The chancel was finally re-roofed and restored by the end of 1603, closing the curtain on this ignoble 17-year episode.[32]

A New Knight in the Neighbourhood

Two years before the court settled the roof case, a parishioner named Robert Sandy removed the carved wooden screen separating the chancel from the nave, presumably to save it from the elements. Sandy had recently purchased Luton Hoo, and soon after changed his surname to *Napier*. His son eventually built a family chapel at the Hoo, and tradition has it that the screen from St. Mary's found its way there. A book by Henry Shaw published in 1830 contains illustrations of this lavishly ornamented chapel.[33] Some of the screens bear a strong resemblance to the one in St. Mary's which divides the Hoo Chapel from the south transept.

In 1605, King James I paid a visit to Sir John Rotherham at Someries Manor. There he met Robert Napier and upon returning home recorded, *Mr. Robert Sandy had a house and land in the parish of Luton, and was a suitable person with whom to negociate a loan.*

King James continued his acquaintance with Napier, visiting him at Luton Hoo in 1611. He later made him a knight and eventually a baronet.

Sir Robert's star was on the rise. The following year, Sir John Rotherham sold property to Napier that included the manor of Luton. Napier already possessed all the lands of the ancient manor.

In 1610 a prosperous farmer, Thomas Attwood, presented the church with a silver communion cup engraved with the words: *Given this cupe to the Church of Luton by Thomas Attwood of Castle Street for Communyan Cupe 1610.*

Attwood's Cup is the earliest surviving of all of St. Mary's vessels, vestments and ornaments. Those from the pre-reformation days were either lost, stolen or sold to pay for repairs. Today the cup is kept in a bank vault and a replica is used in communion services.

After twenty-two years at St. Mary's, Vicar Edmund Brockett took another position and King James I appointed John Birde, B.D. as his successor. An Oxford graduate, Birde had a wife and two children when he came to Luton. He officiated from 1617 until 1644, during which time he baptised 13 of his own children and buried five.

Keeping the Congregation Fit

The year following Birde's induction, King James directed that catechising replace sermons in the Sunday afternoon service. How people responded is unknown, but there's no doubt about their reaction when he published his *Book of Sports* and ordered it to be read aloud in the Church! The publication promoted dancing, archery, leaping and other sports on Sunday afternoons, which particularly offended the Puritans. The official reason for the King's command was to divert people away from worse occupations. In any event, the Puritan Party viewed it as a betrayal by the one who bore the title *Defender of the Faith*.

In 1623, the King sold St. Mary's advowson to Sir Robert Napier, which meant he had the right to appoint future vicars. Napier held the advowson on condition of the knight's service and partial payment of a knight's fee. In other words, King James re-established the military status that William the Chamberlain attached to the advowson in the 11th century.

Sometime in 1629, Sir John Rotherham sold his estate at Someries to Thomas Crawley and his son Francis. The Rotherham family had held the property for over 150 years, ever since Lord Wenlock's death at the battle of Tewkesbury. Now it passed into the hands of the Crawleys, along with the rights to Someries Chapel in St. Mary's. Thomas Crawley died 15 December 1629, and his will directed his body be buried *in my Chapel of Someries in Luton Church*. His carved gravestone can be seen today in the floor of the north transept.

As owners of Luton Hoo, the Napiers were already using the Hoo Chapel for family burials. Sir Robert Napier's will, written in 1635, indicates that his wife was interred in the family vault beneath the chapel and that he wished to be buried near her. Sir Robert died two years later, leaving the church four cottages for the housing of poor people, money for the distribution of bread to the poor after Sunday services, and £10 *to my loving friend, John Burd, our vicar*. (About £700 in today's money.)

As the century progressed, Vicar John Birde, along with knights Robert Napier junior and Francis Crawleybegan sensing tremors on the political and religious landscape. In 1641 they petitioned Charles I to preserve both the Order of Church Government and the Book of Common Prayer. Napier and Crawley were staunchly loyal to the Royalist cause, and the Vicar, who had to be careful of his position, quietly sympathised.

Stripped and Mangled

The same month Napier and Crawley sent their petition to London, the House of Commons dispatched commissioners to deface and remove from churches and chapels *all images, altars, or tabels turned altarwise, crucifixes, superstitious pictures and other monuments and relics of idolatry*. In the hands of fanatics, this activity quickly disintegrated into wholesale destruction. Altar-tombs, brasses, piscinae, Easter sepulchres, and other objects of antiquity were mutilated and irreparably lost.

Smashing stained glass windows was also part of the agenda. Only windows positioned high in the church might be safe, since clergymen were known to refuse commissioners a ladder. Perhaps this is what saved the small treasure of medieval glass that yet survives in the Wenlock Chapel.

Most of the mutilation of St. Mary's occurred during this period rather than the Reformation of the previous century. The Virgin Mary over the high altar was destroyed as well as the high altar itself. The image of the Virgin Mary in the St. Nicholas Chapel, crosses on the rood loft and the green rood, the cross enthroned, and all of the images and altars of St. John the Baptist, St.

Catherine, St. Margaret, St. Sithe, St. George, St. Clement and St. Nicholas were destroyed. Whether the parish complied with the order to remove the communion rails and level the chancel is unknown.

One can only imagine the grief some parishioners felt at seeing St. Mary's stripped and mangled. Others were undoubtedly overjoyed that the church was cleansed at last of what they considered idols. Members from both sides worshipped within her walls and claimed her as their own.

When Loyalty was Scandalous

Civil war loomed on the horizon when Parliament established *The Committee for Scandalous or Malignant Ministers*. Ministers remaining loyal to the King were *malignan*t according to Parliament, who sought to eject them from their positions. The King in turn dismissed ministers loyal to Parliament. While Charles I exchanged punches with Parliament, the clergy took the blows! Two years later in 1642, another committee – this one for *Plundered Ministers* - was formed to assist ministers ejected by the King.

In 1645, the Committee for Scandalous Ministers ejected St. Mary's former Vicar, Edmund Brockett, from his position as Rector of Gravely cum Chisfield, Herts., for his loyalty to the King. He was at least seventy-three years old by then.

The Revd John Birde found himself in a most precarious position. When Civil War finally erupted, he did not come out in overt support of the King. Bedfordshire as a whole backed Parliament, but some of St. Mary's parishioners remained loyal to Charles I, including Napier and Crawley

What actually happened to Birde during the war years is uncertain. Luton neglected to maintain its registers from 1643 until 1647, and Birde made his last entry just weeks before the war began. Furthermore, Bedfordshire clergymen came under pressure to pledge allegiance to Parliament. Local and county committees actively rooted out clergy suspected of loyalty to the monarchy.

Birde relinquished the living at St. Mary's in 1644, but kept his smaller one at Cheddington, perhaps an indication of the stress he was under. Withdrawing from the spotlight of a large parish would have eased his situation.

The sword of dissension cut deep gashes into St. Mary's congregation. Royalists predominantly favoured keeping the Order of Church Government, the Prayer Book and other measures designed to promote reverence for the altar and elements of communion. The Puritans were aligned with Parliament, wanted the Prayer Book abolished and pushed for a greater emphasis on preaching God's Word. Charles I antagonised the Puritans even further by re-ordering churches to read from the *Book of Sports* in their services.

Given the schism in the church, no one would envy Samuel Austin's role as Mr. Birde's replacement. The Central Committee for Plundered Ministers appointed Austin to the position. Normally the patron of the church nominated the Vicar, but Sir Robert Napier forfeited his estates when he declared his loyalty for the King. The patronage came attached to his property, but even when he paid to get his estates back, he was denied the privilege of appointing the Vicar for the duration of the Commonwealth.

A Parish in Pain and Rebellion

Samuel Austin, who held a Master's degree from Oxford, stayed less than two years. An entry in the *Proceedings of the Committee for Plundered Ministers* noted that on 6 December 1645, Austin resigned and that he *desired an especiall care may bee taken for the settling of some godly minister in his steed in regard of the divisions of the said parishe.*

The Committee suggested that Bedfordshire knights and gentlemen desiring a speedy reconciliation should recommend a *godly divine* to take Austin's place. The Justices of the Peace also promised Austin help in recovering tithes and money owed him by the church, which they had refused to pay!

Committee records show that three months later (March 1646) the living was presented to Thomas Atwood Rotherham, *a godly and orthodox Divine who is required forthwith to officiate the cure of the said church as Vicar and preach diligently to the parishioners there.*

Rotherham, baptised at St. Mary's in 1602, had also been a curate under Birde, and was related to the Atwood and Crawley families. Like his predecessor, he failed to resolve the painful division within St. Mary's. He resigned during the nineteen-month period between March 1646 and October 1647. He had previously held appointments as Vicar of Ickelford in Hertfordshire (near Hitchin) and Rector of St. John Zacharies in London. Rotherham mentions these positions on the title page of his book, *A Den of Theeves Discovered*. The work was in response to *certaine errours and false doctrines delivered in a sermon* by a curate in Hertfordshire. In the introduction, Rotherham wrote:

> That which moved me to undertake this worke, was not out of the least thought of any abilitie in my selfe above others, (I speake not by way of humble pride) but I had a challenge given me, with many a jeere and mocke behind my back, when my extreme sorrowes called for better usage.

Rotherham exhorted his readers to not become discouraged by the heretic, adding *God will blast his stinking breath and blesse you with the sweet breathings of His Holy Spirit.* The extreme sorrows he referred to may have been the death of his son, which he mentioned as part of the reason he did not finish the manuscript earlier.

Thomas Rotherham's replacement at St. Mary's was Mr. Carey. Other than his name and the fact that he also resigned before October 1647, nothing is known about him.

A gap exists in the records between 1646 and 1650. If a minister held the appointment during those years, there is no record of his name. It is possible that St. Mary's was without a Vicar during these years.

Just who nominated Thomas Jessop to the post in 1650 remains a mystery. The Committee for Plundered Ministers no longer functioned and Sir Robert Napier was still not permitted to appoint anyone. Jessop's experience with the bitterly divided church was no better than that of the previous intruded ministers (as they were later called), though he persevered longer.

During this period ministers did not need to be ordained, and some parishioners resented the fact that Jessop lacked this qualification. It appears that Sir Francis Crawley, along with Sir Robert Napier and others, retreated from the church, hired their own minister and held services in the chapel at Luton Hoo. In their private facility they could continue using the liturgical form of worship no longer permitted at St. Mary's.

Sir Francis died before the end of 1649, and his wife Elizabeth passed away eight years later. The violence and controversy surrounding her funeral make it one of the more infamous services in St. Mary's history.

The Burial of Lady Crawley

"I am sorry about the death of Lady Crawley, and of course she must be buried next to Sir Francis in your chapel at St. Mary's," the Vicar's note said. "Unfortunately, I cannot allow you to read the burial service from the Book of Prayer in the church. However, you are free to have a minister of your own choosing at the funeral, as long as he limits himself to a word of exhortation."

Thomas Crawley, who had been reading Jessop's reply aloud to his grieving family and friends, crumpled it up and threw it on the floor.

"Mother *will* be buried in our chapel and the service *will* be from the Book of Common Prayer," he vowed furiously.

"How do you suggest we do it then?" challenged his older brother, Francis.

"I say we take the coffin and go now. It's dark outside and the church will be locked. We may have to break down the door but who is going to stop us?" And besides," he went on, "I'm ordained and can perform the service myself. We don't need another clergyman."

Thomas' confidence and zeal ignited the group's long-standing bitterness over the changes in the church. Convinced that their cause was just and right before God, men jumped to their feet to help carry the coffin, and with the women following, they set off for St. Mary's.

The Sexton had been making his final tour of the grounds when he heard the crash of bodies against a door. Running to the sound, he arrived in time to see the group armed with torches disappear into the building. But not before he recognized the Crawleys! He was no match for such an important family, so off he sprinted toward the vicarage 75 yards away.

Alerted by the sexton, Jessop rushed to St. Mary's to find the family gathered around the open tomb and Thomas' finger on the page containing the burial service.

"What is the meaning of this?" he demanded.

"We are burying our mother according to her wishes and our rights," Crawley responded hotly.

"I already told you that you cannot use the Prayer Book service in this church," the minister angrily replied.

"You are nothing but a clown, a scoundrel and a jacke!" Crawley sneered. "Even Oliver Cromwell allows the use of the Prayer Book in London!"

Outnumbered and not given to violence, Jessop saw the futility of further protest. "We will just see what Oliver Cromwell has to say about this," he threatened and stomped out of the church, allowing the Crawleys to finish burying their mother.

True to his word, on 27 May 1658, Jessop sent off a letter to Oliver Cromwell describing the offence and detailing his frustrations at St. Mary's. His condition *being extremely sad and insupportable through the unwearied opposition of the said party*,[34] he requested that Cromwell grant him relief and act to maintain the civil peace.

Although Cromwell did summon Thomas Crawley to London to answer the charges, the Protector died four months later and Crawley escaped prosecution. Jessop apparently remained at St. Mary's until the restoration of the Monarchy in 1660.

Famous Relatives

In spite of such conflicts that eloquently demonstrate the need for a Saviour, God seemed to have a special place in his heart for the church. At least favours continued coming her way. St. Mary's was not only well connected to famous English people, but also became bound with American History at this time.

On 16th June 1660, the daughter of a Luton maltster and a gentleman named Lawrence Washington recited their marriage vows in St. Mary's. Lawrence was the great-uncle of George Washington, the first U.S. president.

However, the arrival of the new Vicar that year, Thomas Pomfret, undoubtedly caused more of a stir in the congregation than did Lawrence Washington. And although no one knew it then, Pomfret would earn the distinction of becoming St. Mary's longest standing Vicar, holding the position for 45 years!

As long as the profound schism still divided the congregation, no man could lead without alienating some of the parishioners. The more extreme Puritans had already withdrawn from the church to form dissenting congregations (Baptists and Quakers). Those remaining at St. Mary's needed a clergyman who commanded respect even from those who disagreed with him. Pomfret was possibly just the man for the job. Sir Robert Napier, once again patron of the church, appointed the new Vicar. Some speculate that Pomfret had been the Napier family minister at Luton Hoo when the family withdrew from St. Mary's.

Pomfret arrived as an unmarried man, but in his first year obtained not only a wife, but also a Master's degree. The couple had numerous children, five of whom died in infancy. One son, John Pomfret, went on to become Vicar of Maulden as well as a published poet.

Dressing the Dead Warmly

Today's society sometimes devalues elderly people, but in the 17th century even the dead were considered useful. An Act of Parliament in 1666 required that all burial clothes be made from sheep's wool, as a way of encouraging the wool trade!

The family of the departed were obliged to present a signed document to Mr. Pomfret stating that all materials used in the burial shroud, suit, sheet or coffin lining had been 100% sheep's wool. The Reverend in turn submitted an affidavit that he had complied with the Act.

Pirates, Pews and Puritans

In the reign of Charles II, it became common to raise funds for special purposes by taking collections in Parish churches. In 1670, parishioners at St. Mary's contributed to a collection for *the redemption of persons being Christians taken prisoner by the Turks and sold into slavery*. Enterprising pirates in the Mediterranean had discovered that kidnapping and enslaving English sailors was a lucrative business. Ten years later, the plate circulated again for the same purpose.

Parishioners also contributed to the rebuilding of St. Paul's Cathedral (destroyed in the great London fire of 1666), the repairing of St. Albans Abbey and the relief of *distressed Irish and French Protestants.*

Graffiti, a problem in every age, appeared in the church in 1678 when the poet John Dryden visited John Pomfret, the Vicar's son. The two carved their initials in one of the vestry pillars. A workman later plastered over the names, however. Pomfret the poet apparently felt compelled to write…he also cut his name into the east side of the chancel pier. It too, eventually disappeared.

Thomas Pomfret, like his immediate predecessors, struggled with parishioners refusing to pay the vicarial tithes. In a two-year period between 1678 and 1680, Pomfret took legal action four times against individuals for the *subversion of tithes*. He managed to resolve one case out of court and won the other three judgments.

Money was not the only motive for going to court, however. In 1681, a squabble arose between two parishioners over a church pew. Thomas Crosse claimed that rights to the pew came with the estate he had purchased at Bramingham. Thomas Cheney saw it differently. Though his father had sold Crosse the estate five years previously, he maintained the pew was built by his ancestor and therefore belonged to him. Off to court they went to have the matter settled.

The verdict came back that the men were to share the pew and the rights to it as long as they stayed at their present residences. The Cross family continued to use the pew until the latter half of the 19th century.

The Rye House plot to overthrow Charles II was discovered in June 1683. Three months later, Pomfret preached a Thanksgiving Sermon *for the Discovering and Defeating the Late Treasonable Conspiracy against His Sacred Majesties Person and Government.*[35] Bristling against those who used religion to justify rebellion and bloodshed, he began:

> It is not unknown to any man who has heard the sermons, or read the books, or remembers the practices

> of all sorts of dissenters from the Church of England, but that they have been a people not only the most ungovernable, but also the most destructive to the peace and dignity and lives of Princes...some hot and troublesome men amongst us, given up to rage and ambition, have torn up the foundations of peace and government, and will endure neither kings, nor their laws...they will make the Christian Religion, the pretence to Rebellion, and for the concernments of God, practise directly opposite to all His commandments...

The dissenters Pomfret refers to were Puritans. The sermon presented the biblical basis for submission to authority and deftly dealt with the question, *Is it ever permissible to rebel against a wicked king?* This convincing discourse demonstrated Pomfret's excellent communication skills.

Pomfret also succeeded as a writer and published a biography of the Countess Dowager of Devonshire, the sister of his friend Lord Aylesbury. In illustrating her virtues, he presented a picture of how the civil war affected clergymen:

> The war had made loyalty poor and sequestration upon the priests of God had reduced the clergy to such lamentable want that they had nothing left to clothe them but their own righteousness; nor anything to feed on but a good conscience and their passive virtues: these our noble lady saw and pitied, and became the succourer of the righteous cause.

Pomfret also published a collection of sermons by Dr. Mark Frank, an Archdeacon of St. Albans. He dedicated it to Sir John Napier, referring to him as *my very good Patron*, to whom he was indebted for his goodness and favours.

An amusing incident occurred when Pomfret preached before the opening session of the spring assizes in Bedford. Pomfret took his discourse from the Old Testament story of Daniel and Shadrach, Meshach and Abednego's refusal to bow to an idol at the command of the King. Upon hearing this, one of the judges leapt from his chair, thinking Pomfret was advocating sedition. Another judge restrained him from attacking the Vicar, who hastily proclaimed his undying loyalty to the crown. Placated, the judge who had misjudged Pomfret's intent, embraced him at the close of the sermon and invited him to dinner.

Hardly a Blemish

A Vicar uncompromising in his convictions couldn't avoid making enemies. Pomfret had several, and when he died in 1705, they prevented his burial in St. Mary's churchyard.[36] In spite of this, a large crowd turned out for his funeral at the Parish Church of Caddington on 10 March. A sermon preached at the service gives insight into the Vicar's character. Mr. A. Humphrey, the Rector of Barton and friend of Pomfret's for almost thirty years, listed his attributes:

> His temper and disposition was a good foundation to build a holy religion upon, his children received the comfort of his tender care and provision, though to his own hindrance; his friends and neighbours found him always affable and courteous, the poor were refreshed with his bounty, and the rich with his counsel and advice; and few tasted the sweetness of his conversation but desired the continuance of it.
>
> If you look into his life and conversion as a Christian, I believe the blemishes of it will appear to be very few, of which I think this is no small evidence, that the very dissenters had so much respect for him...Another

proof of the regularity of his life may be this, that when a diligent inquisition was made into it, there was hardly blemish enough found to ground a libel upon, and that was no moral failure neither.

Humphrey had visited Pomfret the day before his death and found him studying in spite of his weakness and pain, *so intent he was upon doing good to the souls of men.* He also noted that the Vicar prayed daily for those who troubled him, but that when there were opportunities to publicly say what he thought about his oppressors, he never said anything that was *indecent much less unchristian.*

For all the good that could be said about him, Pomfret started a trend at St. Mary's that future generations would call distasteful!

8.
Deformities, Destructions and Daniel Knight's Revenge

If 17th century commissioners damaged St. Mary's beauty by what they removed, some argue that 18th century parishioners did more damage by what they *added* to the building!

In the opinion of historian William Austin, *parishioners were guilty of a deplorable want of appreciation of the beauties of such a glorious monument of ecclesiastical art as Luton Church.*[37] Austin based his criticism partially on people's fondness for erecting galleries in St. Mary's during the 1700's. One visitor later referred to the chancel gallery as a deformity.[38]

Thomas Pomfret started the trend at St. Mary's in 1691 when he received a license to build one for his patron, Sir John Napier. Other galleries appeared in the north and south aisles, under the western arch, and across the aforementioned chancel arch.

In general, churches built these structures in order to enlarge their seating capacity. At St. Mary's, however, they were mostly pew galleries, large enough only for a single, well-to-do family and one or two of their servants.

As new structures developed on the inside of the building, an old one disappeared from the outside. In 1705, St. Mary's said farewell to the stocks located in the churchyard for several hundred years. Still a fashionable mode of punishment, they were not destroyed, but moved to Market Hill.

The Revd Christopher Eaton, M.A., became Vicar of St. Mary's after Pomfret's death and fulfilled that role for thirty-nine years. He acquired a great deal of property in Luton, and used some of it for farming and malting. Unlike his predecessors, he chose not to live in the vicarage, which was still in good condition.

During Eaton's tenure, the church had two services on Sundays – one in the morning and another in the afternoon. Additionally there were services on Wednesdays, Fridays and festival days. Parishioners could partake of Holy Communion four times a year, an increase over the annual medieval celebration.

St. Mary's boasted an impressive collection of memorial brasses by this time. Perhaps there were so many that people took them for granted. In any case, someone proposed melting down a large number of these in order to make a brass chandelier. Today the chandelier has disappeared, but fortunately a few memorial brasses still survive to remind us of the church's spiritual forefathers.

References to a church school date back to 1673, and in 1731 a tin-plate worker named John Richards left his house in trust to *put five poor boys to school with the Master of the Church School.* When the antiquarian Robert Gough visited St. Mary's later in the century, he recorded that a school functioned in the room above the vestry, accessible by a stairway in Someries Chapel.

Mr. Eaton passed away in 1745, followed by his widow a few months later. Both were buried in the church but have no memorial. Sir John Napier appointed George Barnard, M.A. to succeed Eaton. Only thirty years old when he accepted the position, Barnard was already Rector of Knebworth in Hertfordshire.

The Last Word Carved in Stone

In 1747, a member of St. Mary's named Daniel Knight transferred a portion of his property to Mr. Edward Fossey in order to secure an advance. Samuel Marsom, an attorney, drew up the deed of conveyance for Mr. Knight. Marsom was also the nephew of Luton's Baptist minister and a Baptist himself. When the property was reconveyed, Knight publicly accused the lawyer of defrauding him in the process. Marsom threatened to sue Knight for slander unless he published a retraction. A newspaper printed the apology wherein Knight confessed:

> …that the deeds were faithfully drawn, pursuant to the agreement between himself and Fossey; that he perfectly understood the same before they were executed, and was satisfied with them; and that the reports he had made to the contrary were malicious and scandalous; that he apologised to Mr. Marsom and would never offend in like manner again.[39]

While Knight kept his word not to offend in *like manner* again, he devised another way to get even with Marsom. He composed the epitaph inscribed on his tomb:

> Here lyeth the body of Daniel Knight,
> Who all my lifetime lived in spite.
> Base flatterers sought me to undoe,
> And made me sign what was not true.
> Reader take care whene'er you venture,
> To trust a canting false dissenter,
> Who died June 11th in the 61st year
> Of his age 1756

The newspaper that printed the retraction no longer exists, while Knight's tombstone in the north transept endures to insist that he was ill-used. Visitors find it amusing today but one wonders how Marsom responded to it? However the lawyer reacted, Knight was comfortably (one hopes) beyond the reach of lawsuits, and there was not a thing Marsom could do about it.

Who's Who in the Hoo

St. Mary's patron – Sir John Napier – died in 1750, leaving Luton Hoo to his aunt. Miss Frances Napier of Harrow, Middlesex, was the last member of the family to own the Hoo. She left it to her nephew, Mr. Francis Herne, a member of Parliament, who sold it to John, the third Earl of Bute, in 1761. Lord Bute had been Secretary of State, First Lord of the Treasury and Prime Minister, as well as a friend of King George III.

Although the Napiers association with St. Mary's lasted for 160 years and they were buried beneath the Hoo chapel, there are no brass monuments to the family within the church.

Barnard continued as Vicar for 15 years, until he died at the young age of 45 in 1760. He too, is buried in St. Mary's but like the Eatons before him, has no monument.

The Revd William Prior, D.D. replaced Barnard as Vicar. In 1768 he became headmaster of Repton and left Luton. Although he continued to hold the living, the curate, Coriolanus Copleston, carried out the Vicar's duties.

The Revd George Barnard

During Prior's incumbency, a new style of bell ringing came into fashion. Before the Reformation, each bell had a separate purpose. For instance, a certain one would be used at the elevation of the host during Mass, while another might call townspeople to pray for someone dying. Later the bells were rung together as a way of announcing services. Change ringing or ringing the bells in sequence required a greater number of bells. Churches including St. Mary's found they could economize by melting their existing bells and recasting them into eight smaller ones.

John Wesley's Cold Reception

Mr. William Cole, a former High Sheriff of Bedfordshire, rented the vicarage during this period. While Sheriff, his chaplain had been John Wesley and since the two were friends, Cole probably invited the famous evangelist to preach at St. Mary's on 16 January 1771.

Although Wesley was an ordained Anglican minister, not all Anglicans approved of his message. The clerk at St. Mary's not only refused to allow the church bells rung to announce the service, but reportedly would not help Wesley don his robes.

Wesley did not mention these slights when he recorded his experiences at St. Mary's, but he did allude to something meant to discourage people from staying for the entire service. His diary entry reads:

> I set out for Luton. The snow lay so deep on the road that it was not without much difficulty and some danger that we at last reached the town. I was offered the use of the Church; the frost was exceeding sharp, and the glass was taken out of the windows. However, for the sake of the people, I accepted the offer, though I might just as well have preached in the open air. I suppose four times as many people were present as would have been at the room; and about a hundred in the morning. So I did not repent of my journey through the snow.[40]

Around this period, some of St. Mary's congregation began attending the Methodist meeting house on Sundays. Methodists did not want to start a new denomination and still considered themselves members of the Anglican Church.

A Model, Upper-Class Vicar

Although Dr. Prior was away at Repton School, a new Vicar could not be appointed until he died in 1779. When the opportunity came to nominate the next incumbent, the Earl of Bute chose his fifth and youngest son to fill the position. Although only 24 years old, the Hon. William Stuart, M.A. had received an education commensurate with his station in life.

The new Vicar lived at Copt Hall, a house his father built not far from the neglected Someries Manor. Future Vicars would also reside at Copt Hall while Lord Bute was patron of the living.

Due to his high profile and well-known father, St. Mary's Vicar attracted the attention of three writers of the period. The famous biographer James Boswell introduced William Stuart to his friend Dr. Johnson and described him as *a man worthy of being known to Johnson; being with all the advantages of high birth, learning, travel, and elegant manners, an exemplary parish priest in every respect.* Boswell's comment provides insight into what apparently was considered the model Vicar in those days!

Hennington's Directory of Luton in 1785 noted that the incumbent's *great erudition and noble endowments meliorated even the name of Stuart.*

A novelist of the period, Miss Edgworth, commented that Stuart was a man of contradictions. She described him as having the warmest of feelings and the coldest exterior; a silent man yet a non-stop talker when travelling with his father. She especially appreciated his *keen sense of humour and strong imagination.*

Some interesting "improvements" came about in the church while Stuart was Vicar. The east wall of the chancel received a new circular-headed window and someone decided to paint and gild the stone baptistry. Labourers applied plaster and stucco to all the interior stonework as well as the entire exterior of the building except the tower, which alone kept its chequered appearance. Since plaster did not adhere well to the old Totternhoe stone, much of it was hacked off. Stuart also saw to the re-roofing of the chancel. Obviously he had no intention of letting the grass grow under *his* feet!

A Prestigious Post and Famous Wife

With his talents, money and family connections, St. Mary's Vicar bounded up the ecclesiastical ladder, becoming Canon of Windsor in 1793 and Bishop of St. David's two years later.

Stuart remained single while he ministered at St. Mary's. After he left Luton, he married Sophia Margaret Penn, the granddaughter of William Penn, founder of Pennsylvania.

Stuart was still Bishop during Christmas 1799 when he preached a series of sermons before George III. Soon after, the King wrote him:

> Windsor, Dec. 29th, 1799
>
> My Lord,
> The cordial satisfaction I have derived from hearing the five Sermons you have preached during your residence, and that most excellent one at my Chapel on Christmas Day, obliges me to thank you on paper, and to assure you that I shall feel myself most happy when I shall judge it the proper opportunity to advance you to a more lucrative Bishopric; your talents and exemplary conduct would alone stimulate me had I not the additional motive of your being a son of the truest and best friend I ever had, and out of regard to his memory I truly rejoice that he has in the Church, and Army, two sons who will ever reflect credit on the name of Stuart.

> I cannot conclude without expressing my warmest hopes that you will publish some treatise in defence of the Christian Religion.   –George R.

Sincere about the promotion, the King wanted to appoint Stuart the Archbishop of Armagh the following year - the honour that had eluded Thomas Rose in the 16th century. But Stuart was suffering from ill-health at the time, and the King didn't think he should approach him directly on the matter, *as on those occasions men are not able to judge with firmness, but rather view the difficulties that attend any change.*[41] Instead, George III began negotiations through the Royal Nanny! Apart from looking after the King's children, Lady Charlotte Finch was Mrs. Stuart's aunt. His Majesty desired Lady Finch to speak to Mrs. Stuart, who should then tell her husband of the King's intention.

The former Vicar of St. Mary's didn't appear overly keen to accept the position. As the King anticipated, Stuart was concerned about his health and the possible effects the Irish climate might have on him.

George III dashed off another note to the nanny:

> I should not fulfill my duty if I did not in the most explicit manner now call on him to accept of that eminent situation; nor do I think he would show the zeal I know he possesses (for the cause of Religion and Virtue in Ireland) if he does not instantly yield to this fresh communication of my sentiments on this subject.[42]

Apparently the Bishop of St. David's still hesitated, because three months later the King wrote him directly, calling on Stuart in *the most serious manner to accept of that Dignity in Ireland where I know You will do good.*

William Stuart finally acquiesced to the King's pressure and accepted the position of Archbishop. He didn't seem to be a man who desired the power or prestige of the role.

Stuart's earlier appointment to St. David's in 1795, meant that St. Mary's was ready for another Vicar. Although by this time Lord Mount Stuart was patron of the living, he could not choose the new incumbent. When a vacancy occurred due to the elevation of the prior Vicar, the King made the next appointment. George III selected Revd James Russell Deare, LL.B. Although a bachelor when he arrived, Deare married a few months before resigning his position in 1798. Later in life, he published three of his sermons preached before the Assizes of the county of Kent and dedicated them to his friend, the High Sheriff, John Powell.[43]

Aside from acting as chaplain to the High Sheriff, he was also *chaplain in ordinary* to the King.

When Deare resigned, the Earl of Bute nominated his nephew, Stuart Corbet, as the new Vicar. He too came to St. Mary's pulpit as a single man but married a few months into his incumbency. Both his marriage and that of his predecessor's were announced in *Gentleman's Magazine*.[44]

Whether it had to do with criticism, crime or social announcements, St. Mary's press coverage would increase significantly in the next century.

Archbishop William Stuart, St. Mary's Vicar from 1779 until 1795.

9.
The Case of the Missing Vicars

The birth of the 19th century began with a death: that of eighty-four-year-old Coriolanus Copleston, the curate with the most curious name. Copleston fulfilled the duties of a Vicar without the pay for many of his 30 years of service at St. Mary's. He was laid to rest in the centre of the nave.

In contrast to the long-serving Copleston, Stuart Corbet left St. Mary's after six years, exchanging benefices in 1804 with the Revd Charles Henry Hall, D.D.

Dr. Hall, also a Canon of Christ Church, Oxford, had no intention of settling in at St. Mary's. In fact, after his induction he apparently never set foot in the church again. He went on to become Regius Professor of Divinity in 1807, Dean of Christ Church in 1809, and Dean of Durham in 1824. Hall also took his place in the list of St. Mary's authors, publishing numerous theological works. The Revd Daniel Basley, curate for eighteen years, fulfilled the Vicar's duties in his absence.

As a way of celebrating the Peace of 1814 after years of war with France, the congregation made a procession around the perimeters of the Parish. With a diameter of approximately 30 miles, the Parish was the largest in Bedfordshire. People started out on June 7th and upon finishing, assembled in the market place for a feast. Ever conscious of their responsibility to the poor, parishioners distributed the meat of two bullocks and eleven sheep to the less fortunate on that occasion.

Although William Yardley and John Brett are unknown today, they were celebrities as well as churchwardens at St. Mary's during the first half of the century. Sometime between the years of 1814 and 1829, a clock was placed on the church tower bearing their initials. But their real claim to fame lay in a popular rhyme of the day:

> Mr. Wood of Eaton Green,
> Mr. Dines of Farley,
> Mr. Brett's a big man too,
> And so is Mr. Yardley!

The Archbishop of Armagh and St. Mary's former vicar, William Stuart, died tragically on 6 May 1822 when his wife mistakenly poisoned him. According to the story, she gave him medicine intended for external use only. Stuart, who was 67, did not die immediately and attempted to console his wife by scribbling the message: *At all events I could not have lived long, my dear love.* Family members brought his body back to Luton and buried him in the Stuart family vault under the Hoo Chapel.

A Gallery and Garage

The tower clock was not the only new addition to St. Mary's in the first part of the century. In 1822, *Gentleman's Magazine* reported that masons had moved St. Mary's ancient font and baptistry to the south transept in order to make room for a new gallery in the west end. The structure extended from the tower to the third pillar of the nave and provided room for a new organ purchased the following year. Some sources claim that an orchestra graced St. Mary's during this period, consisting of violins, base viols, flutes and clarinets. Supposedly the orchestra and choir performed from the gallery.

A wooden screen beneath the gallery separated the nave from the vestibule of the church. Parishioners coming through the swinging doors under the gallery would notice high square pews with doors lining the aisles and the *triple-decker* – a combined pulpit, reading desk and clerk's desk - standing against the southeast pillar of the chancel arch. The clerk sat at the lowest desk on the floor from where he led the congregation in their responses from the Common Book of Prayer. At the reading desk above the clerk was the Vicar. When it came time to preach, the Vicar moved up to the pulpit to deliver his sermon.

St. Mary's no longer offered sanctuary to thieves, but she did provide it to the town's three fire engines! For 13 years, beginning in 1823, the small manual appliances were housed under the tower.[45] Convenient if the church caught fire, but one wonders if they were ever needed elsewhere during a service?

Pew Status

With the baptistry relocated and the gallery in place, attention turned to the seating arrangement. In 1828, decision-makers threw out the old high square pews and introduced a new scheme featuring first and economy class seating. Poorer parishioners sat on open benches, while sleek oblong pews were provided for the better class folk. At the same time, the Vicar and squires held on to their private pews.

Ten years later the open benches were also scrapped and more pews inserted in their place. But the lower class was still accommodated separately – this time on narrow benches in the centre of the nave.

This kind of class distinction flourished in the church, contrary to the Epistle of James, which expressly forbids seating people according to their economic status. It is a striking example of how Christians in every age are vulnerable to social norms at odds with biblical mandates.

Dr. Hall, officially St. Mary's Vicar for 23 years, held on to the living even though absent. When he died in 1827, John the first Marquess of Bute appointed the Revd William McDouall, M.A. to fill the position. McDouall resided in Luton and lived in Copt Hall.

In 1837, St. Mary's connection with the Diocese of Lincoln came to an end. After more than seven centuries, the church became part of the Diocese of Ely.

Another long-standing tradition, that of holding a school within the church, came to a close after 1838. The school moved to a new building on Church Street, on land donated by the Marquess of Bute.

St. Mary's helped plant a church in 1840 in East Hyde. The Marquess of Bute again generously donated land for the facility, churchyard and vicarage as well as £600 towards the buildings. Mr. McDouall also made a financial contribution. Curates from St. Mary's conducted services at East Hyde for nearly twenty years until a new Parish was formed.

Shocking Devastation

A scathing article criticising both the physical and spiritual condition of St. Mary's appeared in *The Northampton Mercury* in 1847:

> This noble church is in a most disgraceful condition…Our business is not so much with its architectural details as with the injuries it has suffered. The ruinous condition of the western window, so lovely even in its present ruin, led us to expect many flagrant abuses, though it did not at all prepare us for the scene of

shocking devastation which burst on us when we had fairly entered the church.

The chancel, which owing to a deformity suspended across it…is rendered useless and affords a miserable instance of neglect…The Wenlock chapel is in a state of filthy neglect, added to which, it is apparently converted into a school-room, with all its shabby fittings-up, and the dirt which its late occupants had introduced; out of this springs a staircase, much resembling one that would be used in a stable or granary. It leads to a loft which, we were informed, was also a school room…The beautiful western window is hidden from view; its present state shaming those who, we presume, stuck up a gallery for the purpose of concealing it. The introduction of this clumsy contrivance led to the removal of the font, with the interesting baptistry, to the ridiculous position it now occupies…The baptistry is whitewashed, and almost rendered ugly from the glaring effect produced by this wretched stuff; this corner also appeared to be the refuge for dirt, cinders and other defilements. The aisles are in a state of ruin…

If any one were to ask us which of the Bedfordshire churches exhibits most completely everything that is distressing to a true churchman, we should answer "the most beautiful one:" and continue, "Go to Luton, and as you pass along the town you will see, in the vast piles of buildings recently erected for the purposes of trade and commerce, evidences of increasing wealth and prosperity, and you will find the inhabitants showing forth their gratitude to Him from whom these blessings come, by erecting for themselves spacious and substantial mansions, furnished with every contrivance for comfort that the extravagant luxury of the nineteenth century has called forth; and with cold indifference leaving the House of God to crumble into ruins.[46]

The writer blamed the church's state on the *lukewarmness and covetousness of churchmen*, adding that perhaps there had been *as great an inattention to the spiritual wants of the parish as to the fabric of the church.*

In the early morning hours of 10 November 1843, a fire broke out in Luton Hoo, destroying the 200-year-old ornate chapel. Someone managed to save the altar however, and reportedly placed it in the Hoo Chapel at St. Mary's. What happened to it after that is a mystery. Two years later, the Marquess sold the entire estate. Friends of St. Mary's curate, the Revd Thomas Sikes, purchased the advowson, which was sold separately.

Dangerous New Technology

When gas lighting came to Luton, churchwarden William Phillips urged the Vicar to install it in the church. A number of St. Mary's parishioners were beginning to attend evening services at other churches already using gas lighting. But Mr. McDouall did not trust the technology and vetoed the idea, fearing the church would catch fire. Unfortunately, the fire engines were no longer housed under the tower; otherwise the Vicar might have considered it!

McDouall was very much an aristocrat and drove around in a large yellow carriage featuring a coachman up front and two footmen in the back. He left most of the officiating in St. Mary's to his curate Thomas Sikes.

A former mayor of Liverpool, John Shaw Leigh, Esq., moved to Luton when he purchased Luton Hoo in 1848. He set about restoring parts of the mansion destroyed by the fire, including the chapel.

William McDouall died the following year at age 74, and Thomas Sikes' friends, who owned the advowson, appointed him Vicar.

Sikes became the first Vicar in 50 years to take an active role in St. Mary's. The absence of leadership had resulted in more than just a disgruntled congregation. People complained about the poor quality of the music and referred to the church as *eerie, bleak and desolate.*[47]

The new Vicar directed his attention first, however, to making changes in the old vicarage, where he had lived as curate. He enlarged the south end and added spacious dining and sitting rooms. Sikes also purchased several pieces of land adjacent to the south side of the vicarage.

An Order from the Home Office forbade burials in the ancient churchyard after 1 June 1854. A special dispensation allowed burial after that date for those who already had spouses interred there. Subsequent burials took place at the new church cemetary on Crawley Green Road.

Close Call for a Valuable Treasure

After only four years at St. Mary's, Sikes exchanged livings with Thomas Bartlett, M.A., Rector of Chevening in Kent. At age 65, Mr. Bartlett probably did not take into account the ministry demands of such a large parish. Although he resigned three years later, he made significant improvements during his short incumbency. He had the Bute gallery under the chancel arch dismantled, as well as the ones over the aisles. A flat ceiling covering oak beams in the chancel roof also came down.

Workers dismantling the Bute Gallery discovered a hidden treasure wrapped in layers of course woollen material: the old chancel screen decorated with medieval painting. Thinking it worthless, the churchwardens planned to sell the screen for firewood until the architect persuaded them otherwise. He estimated it to be one of the most valuable items in the church. Instead, the churchwardens decided to store it in the south porch where it was used to keep the coal in a heap! An ignoble function for something of such historic value.

Thomas Piele, D.D., an eminent Greek scholar as well as Fellow of Trinity College, Cambridge, and Tutor at University College, Durham, replaced Bartlett. Piele previously served as headmaster at Repton School (1841-54), the second Vicar of St. Mary's to have held that position.

Aside from his other credentials, Dr. Peile was an author. Over 30 of his books and published sermons can be found in the British Library. Some of his books are *Annotations on the Epistles*, *Miracles of Healing Power* and *Sermons Doctrinal and Didactic, Bearing on the Religious Topics of the Day*.

His writing reveals that he was an excellent communicator. He was also generous to the smaller Anglican churches in the districts of East Hyde, Christ Church and Stopsley, giving £456 of his vicarial tithes to their needs.

An uprising in India in 1857 prompted Queen Victoria to call for a day of solemn fasting, humiliation and prayer on 7 October. *The Luton News* reported that

> Devout and attentive congregations assembled in the Parish Church and in Christ Church, both morning and evening, who entered with deep feeling into the very appropriate and pathetic service provided for the day…Revd Dr. Peile preached an impressive sermon in the morning, after which a liberal collection in aid of the fund for relieving the sufferers was made.

Bungled Burglary

Shortly after midnight in September 1860, a Luton police constable saw two men acting suspiciously in the neighbourhood of St. Mary's. An account of what followed appeared a few days later in *The Bedford Times*:

> Desperate Encounter with Burglars
> Great sensation was caused in Luton on Tuesday morning last in consequence of the capture of two notorious burglars by the police, whilst in the act of plundering the vestry room of the parish church. It appears that police-constable Dorrington was on duty on Monday night, when a little after midnight he observed two suspicious-looking characters walking along one of the streets. After watching their movements some time, he felt satisfied they were thieves and contemplated committing some unlawful act before morning. He communicated with some of his brother officers in the adjoining beats, and in a few minutes police-constables Neville, Jaquest, and Armstrong made their appearance. Dorrington and the other officers then went towards the church, that being the direction taken by the two men. The door of the church being found open. On going inside the officers found that an entry had been made to the vestry-room, and skeleton keys were in the lock of the door. On looking in and discovering the two men in the act of breaking open a cupboard and a desk, the officers rushed in to make a capture; but before they could carry out their intentions the burglars became aware of their presence, seized their bludgeons and made a fearful attack on the pursuers. Two of the officers were knocked down as they went up, when the thieves were immediately confronted by the other two, upon whom

also they inflicted severe bruises, by their heavy and dangerous instrument. The struggle lasted some minutes, and we regret to state that Jaquest was seriously injured on the head from blows inflicted by a life preserver. The thieves were at length mastered, handcuffed, and safely lodged in the lock-up. The officers afterwards returned to the church and made further examination, where they found a large quantity of jemmies, skeleton keys, crow-bars, centre-bits, etc. In a shrubbery near the church, the officers found a carpet bag which contained a considerable stock of first-class housebreaking instruments.

The prisoners were taken before J.S. Crawley, Esq., on Tuesday, and were remanded to the Petty Sessions on the following Monday. The names of the men, as far as can be ascertained, are Geo. Bennett, alias Bonner Bennett, alias Henry Simpson, 23 years of age, of Bedmead, King's Langley, Herts, and Henry Lee, aged 27, who describes himself as an engineer, and a native of Birmingham. Judging from the large quantity of house-breaking instruments and bludgeons found in and near the church, the police are of opinion that the gang numbers more than the two men captured, at all events, preparations had been made for transacting business to a great extent; but it is a fortunate circumstance that their season, for this year at least, has so suddenly closed.[48]

The *Luton Times* also reported the story, noting that *three of the police are frightfully bruised, as are the two prisoners, so much so that they could not be taken before the magistrates for examination, nor were the police officers in a fit state to give evidence.*[49] A surgeon had to be summoned to attend to injured constables and prisoners.

Prior to his incumbency at St. Mary's, Dr. Peile had purchased the advowson. Although ministers couldn't appoint themselves to a church, they could legally transfer an advowson to a family member or a trustee who in turn would nominate them at the next vacancy. Apparently this is what Dr. Peile did. But being a scholar and schoolmaster, he had difficulty adapting to his new role as Vicar. He stayed four years before relinquishing the work to the Revd George Quirk, M.A. Dr. Peile accepted the perpetual curacy at St. Paul's, Hampstead and later became Rector of Buckhurst Hill in Essex.

Quick Work of Quirk

George Quirk was a round-faced, beardless man with a brisk personality. His tenure at St. Mary's proved brisk as well, lasting only fourteen months. During that time, however, he participated vigorously in the life of the parish and various organisations, especially the Young Men's Christian Association for Mutual Improvement. He also gave a series of lectures refuting Mormonism, which *The Luton Times and Dunstable Herald* promoted:

> The Revd G. Quirk will follow up the success of his first attack on this system by a second lecture on Tuesday evening next. The extraordinary audacity of the author of the *Book of Mormon* and the impious pretensions he puts forth were so fully and clearly explained and exposed at the previous lecture that the crowded assembly listened to the voice of the talented lecturer with feelings of gratitude and admiration. Again will the Vicar bring the powers of a vigorous mind and informed intellect to bear on the astounding assumptions of the Latter-day Saints. The excitement manifest at the previous lecture and the densely crowded state of the room have induced the committee to make all possible provision for a very large audience as it is anticipated that the room at their disposal will be fully occupied. As the object of the lectures is not in the remotest sense a pecuniary one but as they are intended to diffuse information and cripple the

exertions of Mormon preachers, there will be no charge for admission. A collection will be made to defray incidental expenses.[50]

Just a few weeks prior to that particular piece, the same newspaper announced Mr. Quirk's intention to resign due to the *continued disadvantages attending a bad state of health*. They added that *the decision has not been arrived at without mature deliberation, but will nevertheless be received by a great majority with feelings of sorrow.*[51]

George Quirk was well liked. His friends sent him off with a engraved silver inkstand: *Presented to the Revd George Quirk in testimony of his catholic spirit and kindly nature, by a few friends, on his leaving Luton, April 1862.* The newspaper reported the event, noting:

> The addresses delivered on the occasion were expressive of the sentiments of the parishioners respecting the amiable character and the valuable services of the late Vicar. The Revd Quirk…referred to the kindness and sympathy he had experienced from the various Christian communities in the town during his residence among us. He alluded in graceful terms to the readiness with which the ministers of other churches had co-operated with him, and he hoped that the good feeling and Christian unity existing among the various religious bodies might be extended to his successor as it had to him. He said that when he first came to Luton he had to work out a way for himself into the affections of the people, but for his successor the way was in some degree prepared. He hoped that the town, which to him would ever be associated with pleasing reminiscences, would morally, spiritually and commercially flourish and prosper.[52]

The Galloping Vicar

The man who next purchased the advowson became one of the church's most forceful and controversial Vicars. Three monuments in the church speak of the high regard in which parishioners held the Revd James O'Neill. But a good number also considered him a bully. Ambitious, motivated and genuinely concerned for the parish, O'Neill had a volatile temper. Like his 16th century predecessor, John Gwynneth, the Vicar fought several battles in court.

Mr. O'Neill began his ministry as a missionary to Ceylon (present day Sri Lanka). He and his wife, Elizabeth, worked under the auspices of the Church Missionary Society, but after two years on the field, Elizabeth died. Her husband and two young sons stayed another seven years, not returning to England until 1855.

The Revd James O' Neill

When the Vicar first arrived, Luton's population was 18,000 and growing rapidly. People became accustomed to seeing O'Neill dash around the large parish in a four-wheeled-gig pulled by his black mare, Bessie. They began calling him *the galloping vicar*!

Aside from duties that drew him outside the church, the inside of the deteriorating building also demanded his attention. Early in his tenure he noted that:

> ...no person with architectural taste could enter the church without feeling that the removal of the baptistry from its proper place and the erection of the gallery were alterations in the wrong direction, and that if the whole of the internal structures were cleared away, and the church

left to exhibit its original grand proportions, it would be an unquestionable gain.[53]

In a sermon on the text from Haggai 1:8 - "Build the temple that I may take pleasure in it and be glorified," - O'Neill exhorted his congregation to consider their responsibility for restoring St. Mary's:

> Let me remind you that this material temple in which you are now assembled has claims from its conditions which each one ought to hasten to recognise...It is not fit, it is not right, that the mother church of the parish should continue in a state which all lovers of what is beautiful must condemn, but which every right-minded person must deplore. It is hoped that everyone who does not take the very selfish view of 'allowing posterity to take care of itself,' will render assistance by every means in his power.

O'Neill's passionate oratory ignited the parishioners, who formed a committee to raise funds and then hired the well-known architect, G.E. Street to draw up a report on the necessary restorations.

Street's report, written in May 1864, estimated that it would take up to £11,000 to restore the church. Sceptics thought the expense too great and doubted the restoration would ever take place.

Cautious people often marvelled at the hugeness of his financial schemes, a journalist wrote of O'Neill, *but somehow, when the Vicar started about getting money or anything else, his foresight and generalship invariably brought him through.*[54]

A Welcome Destruction

In the *Parish Magazine* of January 1865, O'Neill wrote:

> The work of restoration has at last begun in earnest. On Monday the 9th, the nave and aisles were delivered into the hands of the contractor, who, in 24 hours, had so far proceeded with the work of demolition that the interior presented little else than a pile of straggling wood. There are so very few acts of a destructive kind, which can give so little regret as this must do…It is hoped that a good work thus begun will never be allowed to rest for lack of funds.

Unfortunately, lack of funds and lawsuits did hinder the work; but everything Street proposed was eventually accomplished.

The massive undertaking of the interior renovations took twenty years to complete. Thick coats of cement were removed from the pillars, arches and walls. Then the exposed stonework needed to be polished. These were just the initial steps to restoring the nave. To lay tiles, the floor had to be covered in concrete. But first, human remains buried in the church were exhumed and either re-interred or placed in the crypt *under the north transept which was not filled in.*[55]

By 1888, the interior renovations were completed, with the exception of the windows in the Wenlock and Hoo Chapels. On November 19th that same year, Mr. H. Cobbe, Rector of Maulden, delivered a lecture at the church on the History of St. Mary's. He went on to write a 600-page book on the subject, published posthumously in 1899. A hundred years after its publication, it remains the most complete work on the history of the church, though it is unfortunately out of print.

Trouble Behind the Scenes

As the beautification of St. Mary's progressed, relationships behind the scenes were deteriorating. Vestry meetings often sizzled with tension and hostility over O'Neill's refusal to appoint a suitable churchwarden, his reluctance to hand over receipts and records when appropriate, and a host of other issues.

Even worse, O'Neill and his opponents began airing their disagreements in *The Luton Times*. Through letters to the editor, the men shook their fists at each other, defending their own actions and accusing others of impertinence, illegal activity and unflattering motives. Various demands and impressive threats added to the drama and probably delighted the non-church-going public.

The years 1867 and 1868 are particularly sad in this respect. The *Luton Times and Dunstable Herald* featured headlines such as: "Church Warden Locked out of Vestry;" "Criminal Proceedings for the Libel against the Revd James O'Neill;" "Charge of Assault against Revd J. O'Neill;" "The Queen v. O'Neill," and "J.S. Crawley, Esq., v. Revd J. O'Neill."

The accusation of assault appeared the most serious. Leading up to the event, Churchwarden Samuel Oliver and O'Neill had been at each other like two pit-bulls. What actually happened has never been resolved with certainty. Oliver claimed that O'Neill pushed him across the vestry room several times, called him a scoundrel and vagabond and insisted that he leave. Both men had come to count the offering, but O'Neill maintained that Oliver *seized and pocketed the gold and silver nearst to him, which had been given in the house of God for a special purpose and should therefore be sacred to that purpose.*[56] The Vicar vehemently denied laying hands on Oliver and calling him names.

To those who did not understand the situation, it appeared that O'Neill was accusing his churchwarden of theft. He was not. Rather it was a disagreement over where the money should be directed. Oliver felt obliged to apply it toward one expense and O'Neill insisted otherwise.

The Vicar had enough legal trouble with Oliver, but then he complicated matters by slandering the Churchwarden's lawyer. In a letter to the editor, O'Neill wrote that he should expect little else from Mr. Shepherd than *a tissue of falsehoods*. The lawyer felt that such an opinion by a prominent person in the community could hurt his business. He gave O'Neill the choice of publishing an apology or going to court.

A Humiliating Position

O'Neill did publish another letter, but not to apologise. They went to court. The Vicar was found guilty of slander and the judge delivered the sentence:

> James O'Neill, I shall not aggravate the humiliating position in which you now stand by many observations of my own. I can only say that the libel is one of a very serious character imputing to the defendant an habitual disregard of truth, in other words, a want of the first requisite in the character of a gentleman and a man of honour. I trust I shall not betray my duty in not inflicting upon you a sentence to which by law you are liable, one of imprisonment. The sentence of the court is that you pay to the Queen a fine of £50, and that you be imprisoned until that fine be paid.[57]

The Vicar immediately paid the fine.

O'Neill was never actually charged with assaulting the churchwarden. Oliver's lawyer applied to have the charge brought against the Vicar but the Court of Queen's Bench dismissed the application. The men continued fighting through the columns of *The Luton Times* about other matters.

One gentleman, who did not approve of carrying out controversies through a newspaper, finally could control his pen no longer and published the following letter to O'Neill:

> Sir, I deeply regret you are so fond of writing in newspapers. I think if you had never put your pen to paper since you have resided in Luton, you would have

had cause for rejoicing, for it appears impossible for you to pen a letter without leaving a sting behind and making enemies...The first time I saw you was when I joined my neighbours to take a farewell of Mr. Quirk, your predecessor; we parted with pain and regret, but had the future been known to us on that occasion our visit would have been painful indeed. The parish was then in peace and harmony, and now see the state of things, and ask yourself, *is there not a cause?* Look at it as you found it, and look at it now. You say those who refuse to attend the Parish Church are actuated by folly and perverseness, were they perverse before you came? You have had as churchwardens Mr. Crawley, Mr. Shepherd, Mr. Pearman, and Mr. Oliver, and you have disagreed with the whole of them. We formed a committee and raised funds to put the churchyard in repair, but your conduct defeated our intention. Is the perverseness all on the part of the people? May it not be with yourself? ...Trusting that this will be the last time I shall have to address you through a public newspaper, I am, your obedient servant, W. Willis.[58]

In view of the turmoil in the 1860's, the three monuments to O'Neill in the church are puzzling. Furthermore, the outpourings of grief at the Vicar's death and the testimonies to his greatness were numerous and apparently genuine. There are probably several reasons for this. In spite of the controversy embroiling his earlier years, the Vicar was a talented and forceful man who could get things accomplished. And while his faults were glaringly obvious to the entire community, he performed many kind and generous acts secretly. There is also evidence suggesting that he mellowed during his thirty-four years at St. Mary's and regretted his earlier actions.

O'Neill did much to improve the music in the services as well as eliminate the seating according to class. He championed the cause of education and while he opposed the establishment of a School Board, he was elected to it and served twice as its chairman. O'Neill was also the driving force in the establishment of both St. Matthew's and St. Paul's, as well as the erection of a church hall for St. Mary's.

Towards the end of his incumbency in 1889, O'Neill found himself at odds once again with his churchwardens. John Smith, the church organist who happened to be blind, had retired and left the post vacant. The churchwardens favoured a particular candidate, while O'Neill had been impressed with an enthusiastic 22-year-old. To the disgust of his churchwardens, O'Neill went ahead and hired the young man, Fred Gostelow. Mr. Gostelow remained St. Mary's organist for the next fifty-three years.

End of an Era

During the last months of O'Neill's life, the newspaper printed regular updates about his declining health. The Vicar knew he was dying and planned his funeral, picked out his gravesite, and even wrote a sermon to be read after his death.

O'Neill died at 3:20 am on December 28, 1896. Thirty minutes later a tolling bell at St. Mary's announced the news to the town. Words such as *active, conscientious, vigorous personality, faithful, a safe guide, a man to inspire confidence, of great force of will and strong determination, kind and pleasant*, were some of the adjectives used to describe him in the hours following his death.

A neighbour wrote:

> Luton has lost a venerable servant by the death of its sturdy Vicar, and I venture to say that few in the town or county who know his worth and work will be other than deeply sorry that they shall see his face and hear his voice no more, either in his capacity as a pastor and preacher of the gospel, or as a speaker in defence of his citizen rights and those principles and Institutions he

held so dear. None could doubt his courage, determination, and the fearlessly earnest life. None now will judge meanly of him. As a clear thinker, a devoted worker, an ungrudging giver, a powerful advocate, and as an able organizer and administrator his was a personality of which any town might be justly proud. I fully believe, in the days to come, when time shall have softened down some features of his great character, his works, ways and successes will cause his memory to be venerated, and he will be regarded as the good old Vicar of Luton...[59]

O'Neill was laid to rest on a hill in the church cemetery. Inscribed on the large stone cross marking his grave are words reportedly uttered on his deathbed:

Amid much that was full of failure and full of unworthiness, I have sought to preach the everlasting Gospel of Jesus Christ, upon whose full atonement I shall stand complete before God.

The following year, the Vicar's son Henry Edward O'Neill, donated a stained glass window in the north transept as a memorial to his father. The window commemorates four men who significantly impacted the church as either founders or restorers: King Ethelstan (founder of the Saxon church), Robert Earl of Gloucester (founder of the Norman church), John de St. Alban's (first perpetual Vicar of Luton), and Lord Wenlock (builder of the chapel). Placed into the window are two medallion portraits of James and Elizabeth O'Neill.

Another monument to O'Neill's memory also contains his likeness and was unveiled in 1898. It is a commemorative tablet located on the north wall of the chancel.

Loss of the Historic Vicarage

The Revd Edmund R. Mason, M.A. of Queen's College, Oxford, filled the vacancy left by O'Neill's death. Mason received the appointment from the Peache Trustees,[60] who now possessed the advowson. Before moving to Luton, the new Vicar began a controversial campaign to tear down the old vicarage. He noted that if his request for new accommodation were refused, *I shall be compelled to definitely decline the change of Parish as I should feel it wrong to risk the health of my family.*[61]

The Revd Edmund Mason

Mason, aware that members of the congregation wanted to preserve and renovate the historic vicarage, contracted a sanitary engineer to evaluate the house. The report of the engineer supported his opinion.

In the meantime, St. Mary's parishioners fired off a petition to the Archbishop of Canterbury. They asked the Archbishop to deny Mason's application to sell the vicarage and grounds for the following reasons:

> -That this site has been occupied by the residence of the Vicars of this Parish since 1219 and the present building thereon is of very considerable age. This though a sentimental reason is to our minds a very sufficient one especially in a distinctly modern town such as this.
> -That it is adjacent to the Church precincts is a matter of very practical import in the working of a Parish; and no other suitable residence or land for erecting such is known to be purchasable within easy reach of the Church, the nearest available land being a full quarter of a mile off in the adjoining Parish.

-That the use proposed to be made of the ground by the Corporation namely as a stone yard and slabing and for electric light works will produce a state of things not conducive to the comfort of Worshippers at the services of the church.

-That the reasons given for its sale by the Vendors, namely that it is situated at a low level by the riverside and is consequently unhealthy and that its present condition is certified by the Diocesan Surveyor and also by another expert on behalf of the Vicar to be insanitary are fully met by the following considerations:

-That present day scientific skill is fully capable of rectifying any such defects in its sanitary condition especially as

-an already commenced town drainage and storm water disposal scheme costing £40,000 will shortly lower the level of the water in the soil, render flooding of the curtilage by heavy storms improbable and also provide for the easy discharge of the sewage from the premises and

-the sum paid by the estate of the late Vicar (who lived there 35 years) places the new Vicar in a position to meet any rate a great part of the necessary cost of making its condition sanitary.

We are the more compelled to appeal to Your Grace seeing that the Parishioners as a body have not been consulted on the subject. We humbly submit to Your Grace that it will be a great grief to us as well as a real misfortune if this which has been part of the Patrimony of the church in this Parish for over 600 years should thus be irrecoverably alleviated, a loss not only to us now but one which will be more keenly felt by succeeding generations.[62]

In spite of their pleas, the Archbishop approved the sale of the vicarage, and the proceeds went to purchase property for a new vicarage on St. Anne's Hill, Crawley Green Road.

I will take this opportunity of saying a word about myself, began Mr. Mason on his first Sunday as St. Mary's Vicar. He proceeded:

> In the providence of God the spiritual work of this your noble and beautiful church and of your parish has been offered to me…Depending upon the grace of God, I have accepted the charge, and I stand here today as your minister for Christ…I shall not, my brethren, be influenced by any personal seeking; not be influenced to seek my own pleasure, but rather be guided by principle. My desire will be to uphold that sacred truth, the holy ministry which has been entrusted to me, and to promote our spiritual good. God grant that there may be between you and I, as between minister and people, unity, sympathy, and charity, and then God will give His blessing.[63]

Thus, under the leadership of Mr. Mason, St. Mary's embarked on the final 100 years of the second millennium. What a century it would turn out to be!

The historic vicarage before it was torn down at the end of the 19th century. St. Mary's is in the background.

10.
A Church for All Centuries

When the Revd Edmund Mason inquired about Lord Wenlock in the 20th century, his interests were not purely historical. In 1902, the crumbling Wenlock Chapel prompted the Vicar to investigate ways of funding repairs. He managed to locate the current Lord Wenlock who lived at Escrick Park, York, and told him of the need. Almost five hundred years after his ancestor built the chapel in St. Mary's, Lord Wenlock wrote:

> Sir, I had heard of the Wenlock Chapel in your church but am uncertain as to its erection and maintenance in the past. Has our family been in any way responsible for it? I am afraid from what you say that it requires a considerable sum of money spending on it which will be quite beyond my means. But perhaps you could tell me if any estimate has been made of the necessary outlay.   -Yours truly, Wenlock[64]

Mason directed his churchwarden to provide the information requested and include a photo of the chapel, but there is no record of any further communication between Lord Wenlock and the Vicar.

The chapel may not have been the only thing decaying during this period. Human remains lying in close proximity to the furnace prompted the following letter:

> Dear Mr. Pilgrim,
> Do you know the entrance to the Wenlock mausoleum is now open? Would not it be better now this opportunity is here, of having it cleaned and restored – it might be very useful.
> It has been used as a charnel house to put the human remains which have been found in the churchyard during drainage etc., at different times. These it seems should be properly interred instead of remaining in close chamber near to the furnace – which cannot be any too healthy under the church. Our attention too should be carefully directed to any opportunity of identifying the burial of Lord Wenlock here by careful inspection. I was down at Tewkesbury Abbey sometime last year where Lord Wenlock has long supposed to be buried – but this is now quite contradicted. The tomb and monument there is a century earlier in architecture than his day and there are no records of his being buried there. A paper had then been recently read by an antiquary which stated that Lord Wenlock was buried in his fayre chapelle at Luton Church…
> Yours very truly,
> Mr. E.C. Lee[65]

Mr. Lee was correct. Abbey architects later concluded that what was called the Wenlock Tomb belonged to someone else. The tradition at Tewkesbury is that Wenlock's family collected his body and took it back to Luton for burial. Whether anyone followed up on Mr. Lee's request to investigate the remains in the crypt is difficult to say.

While the interior restorations to the church had been completed by the late 1800's, the exterior work remained to be tackled. In order to raise funds to restore the tower in 1907, the congregation planned an ambitious and complex event: that of re-creating Palestine in Luton! According to the *Luton Times*, it was perhaps the most interesting and instructive exhibition that has ever come to Luton.

> Indeed, any Lutonian who misses this exhibition will miss an educational treat for here one can see more of the curios of the Holy Land than in a six months' tour over the actual country.[66]

Parishioners rebuilt Jerusalem's streets in Plait Hall, including shops, bazaars and alleyways. Dressed in appropriate costumes, members of St. Mary's ran the shops and sold food and articles from Palestine. The event extended beyond Plait Hall to include a concert of Eastern Music, demonstrations of indigenous musical instruments such as a ram's horn trumpet, and lectures on several of the biblical cities. There was even a magic lantern show featuring slides from the Holy Land. The exhibition lasted an entire week in November and succeeded not only in raising money for the tower, but also public interest in St. Mary's.

The Reverend Edmund Mason, who had replaced O'Neill, left the church in 1910. His campaign to tear down the historic vicarage did not appear to hinder his relationships or ministry. As a going away gift the congregation presented Mr. and Mrs. Mason with a piano. A letter of thanks from the parishioners gives a glimpse of the Vicar's character and accomplishments:

During your residence amongst us the various Societies in operation when you came have gone steadily forward, other fields of usefulness have been opened up and received your fostering care, and the tower, roofs of the nave and transepts of our grand old church have been restored.

The example you have set of unwearied devotion and of self-sacrifice, your interest in all good work, your kindly thought for others, and your constant visitation of the sick and poor will ever be held in grateful remembrance.[67]

Tennis and the Titanic

The Revd Arthur E. Chapman, M.A. came from Bristol to fill the vacancy left by Mason. The annual Statement of Accounts for his first year reveals that St. Mary's sponsored a tennis tournament replete with strawberries and cream! It also noted that *Mr. Bonner has worked out a list of vicars back to Morcar the last Saxon vicar, and placed it on the wall of the North Aisle.*

A member of the Society of Genealogists of London undertook the ambitious task of recording the inscriptions on the 192 monuments in St. Mary's Churchyard. The earliest inscription still legible, though barely, dated from 1728. Mr. A. Weight Matthews published all the inscriptions in a series of seven weekly instalments in *The Luton Times* beginning November 21, 1913.

The Revd Arthur Chapman

The collection plates made a special circuit around the church also in 1913, when parishioners moved by the sinking of the Titanic took a collection to help the injured survivors of the tragedy.

In spite of the generous giving towards special needs, it is a rare clergyman who does not have to urge his flock to meet their financial obligations to the church. Chapman was no exception, and in the Statement of Accounts for 1914, he exhorted:

> Ask yourself the question, "Am I bearing my full share of financial responsibility?" If the answer is the negative it means not only that you are leaving the burden to others, but, what is far more serious a matter, it means that your love for and gratitude to Almighty God are not what they ought to be.

Obviously the age of *forgotten tithes* had not completely disappeared, but neither were people keeping such exact accounts!

That same year St. Mary's said goodbye to Ely and became part of the diocese of St. Albans.

World War I broke out in the latter half of 1914 during Chapman's incumbency. The Sunday after Britain entered the war, the Vicar sought to encourage his people from Psalm 46, which begins, "God is our refuge and strength, a very present help in trouble."

> I cannot say much to you this morning. We are all far too anxious about what is going to happen: but I would suggest that you spend much time in prayer to Almighty God. I would suggest that you try to realise that in God we have a defence which can keep us unstained while the enemy threatens us so dreadfully on all hands.[68]

Face Lift for Wenlock

When the west gallery came down in the previous century, the organ was relocated to the Wenlock Chapel. Just prior to the war, someone proposed moving it to the Hoo Chapel. Rights to both chapels belonged to Lady Wernher, owner of Luton Hoo. She not only agreed to the proposal, but also decided to restore the Wenlock Chapel in memory of her late husband, Sir Julius. The restoration involved covering the walls with clunch stone, adding a new roof, reredos, and a communion table. Velvet curtains hung on either side of the reredos. The chapel also contained a cross, vases and a book-rest of silver ornamented with amethysts and rock crystal. The piscina and niche were restored and the century-old axe marks, possibly made by a reformer, disappeared in the process. In total, the cost of the restorations came to six thousand pounds.

Pre-reformation stained glass, previously stored in the church museum,[69] was re-inserted into the upper portion of the chapel's eastern window, and fragments of memorial brasses were placed into the walls.

The Bishop of St. Albans came to dedicate the restored chapel on 24 January 1915, and the festal services continued through the week until the following Sunday.

With the war still in progress, Luton held a memorial service at St. Mary's on 1 November 1917. According to the newspaper, *the bells were rung half muffled as a token of respect to the fallen soldiers and sailors in the Great War. For morning service, 462 changes were rung, and during the afternoon a quarter peal, consisting of 1,260 changes were rung in 50 minutes.*[70]

Mr. Chapman continued at St. Mary's until after the war in 1921 when the Revd Charles Mollan Williams, M.A. replaced him.

The Revd C. Mollan Williams

Sportsmen in the Church

Prior to coming to Luton, Williams had worked with the Church Missionary Society. During his incumbency, an annual Sportsmen's Service took place in the church. On February 26, 1925, *The Luton News* noted that although the attendance that year was disappointing, the service was elevating. The Vicar conducted the devotional preliminaries and the Chairman of the Luton Town Football Club, Harry Arnold, who also happened to be a Councillor, read the lesson.

A gifted young solicitor named Harold Cooke started a Bible Class during this period that metamorphosed into the St. Mary's Boy's Club. Boys would come for the good Bible teaching as well as the football, billiards and other activities. The club attracted 15 and 16-year-old boys who went on to become members of St. Mary's, sidesmen, members of the Parochial Church Council (PCC) and even churchwardens.

Towards the end of Williams' tenure, a young man wandered into St. Mary's to see for himself what went on in the ancient church. He was not a Christian, but because he had attended a church school, Len Ridd understood the "language." He found that he loved the cadence of the 1662 liturgy, decided to stay, and later he accepted the Faith.

Ridd had not been attending St. Mary's very long before Mr. Williams retired due to ill health in 1928. Replacing him was the Revd Richard Thomas Howard, another missions-minded Vicar. Howard was a Cambridge graduate who had served in India with the Church Missionary Society, the same organisation O'Neill had worked with in Ceylon.

The Revd R.T. Howard

"Richard Howard was a most wonderful man," remembers Len Ridd. "He was very modern-minded and a scholar. He was also a rower at University and had several of his oars mounted on the wall of the vicarage."

A Venue for Entertainment

Luton did not have much to offer in the way of entertainment, and television and radio did not yet exist. For centuries, the church provided many of the community's social activities. Dances organised in the Church Hall, for instance, drew large numbers of young people.

In 1931, a group of fifteen parishioners including Ridd formed the St. Mary's Players - a daring move since many churchgoers still considered the theatre a tool of the devil. The forward-thinking Howard was supportive of the group though, whose purpose was simply to produce a good class of plays.

What did the older members of the congregation think of the idea? They must not have been too horrified because they attended the productions.

"Older people were invited to the dress rehearsals for free," said Mr. Ridd. "It was a bit off-putting, however. Some of them were hard of hearing and would loudly ask each other, *What did he say, dear?*"

Most of those who lived around the church were working class people who attended the Evensong service. While seating according to economic status had long been abolished, class differences still mattered. Generally, St. Mary's neighbours did not feel comfortable attending the 11 o' clock Matins, which predominantly attracted Luton's upper-class merchants. Because the neighbourhood people preferred modern hymns played on a piano, St. Mary's provided them with a facility known as *the mission church*, where they could attend Sunday morning services.

No Empty Seats

Although Mr. Howard stayed less than four years, his tenure included several highly successful events, all enthusiastically reported in *The Luton News*. First, the Sunday School Anniversary in May 1931, in which the Morning service featured a procession made up of the choir, Sunday School children and young people from the Bible classes. They marched in through the west door singing *At the name of Jesus every knee shall bow*. The afternoon service was devoted entirely to the children who filled the nave, and still later that day a thousand people attended the Evensong service.

A Choir Festival held at St. Mary's in September 1931 turned out to be *a remarkably inspiring service*, according to *the Luton News*. The festival consisted of 12 choirs made up of 500 singers from South Bedfordshire churches. They filled the chancel, transepts and front half of the nave, leaving the rest of the church for the audience. People lined up at the doors an hour before the service began. Revd William Howard officiated and the Archdeacon of Bedford, A.H. Parnell, preached from Revelation 14:3 about the role of music and singing in Heaven.[71]

The Harvest festival that same year was also a great success, with attendance larger than it had been for several years. Children and young people brought their gifts of fruit and flowers to the afternoon service where they were received at the chancel steps. The Evensong service drew a crowd of 1,300, and additional chairs were brought in to accommodate everyone. The next morning, a group arrived at the church to divide up and allocate the produce to approximately 200 sick and poor people of the parish.

Strangely absent that year is any recognition of the 1,000-year anniversary of the consecration of King Ethelstan's stone church in 931 AD. Why such a momentous occasion was overlooked is a mystery.

Enid Pearce was only five years old when, on behalf of the infant Sunday School class, she presented the Revd R.T. Howard with his going away gift. No one realised it then, but this small act of leadership foreshadowed much bigger things for the future of both St. Mary's and the little girl.

Blame it on the Music

The next significant event of the decade was the institution of the Revd William Davison in July 1933. Davison, who later became a Canon, inherited a very active congregation. St. Mary's numerous organisations included a Parish Church Fellowship, Young People's Fellowship, Bible Classes for older girls, younger girls, women, young men and youths, Men's Conference, Men's Institute, Bible Reading Fellowship, Mother's Union, Choir, Bell Ringers, Girl's Friendly Society, Boy's Club, Football Club, Rangers, Guides, Cubs, Brownies, Scouts and St. Mary's Players.

The Revd William Davison

Davison met with the churchwardens soon after his appointment as Vicar.

"I asked them if they could account for the great congregations. Their immediate reply was, 'The music. We owe so much to Mr. Gostelow and the choir.' "[72]

Davison may have been impressed with the size of the congregation, but he saw no reason to rest on the status quo. Since Mr. Gostelow seemed to be a key to the equation, the Vicar collaborated closely with him. As a result, the eleven o'clock Matins service grew to 400 people and the 6:30 Choral Evensong to 900.

A Rigged Vote

In 1935, Len Ridd, already Secretary of the Young People's Fellowship, was elected to the Parochial Church Council. To the idealistic Ridd, older members of the council seemed stuck in their ways. The following year he devised a scheme to get five of his peers elected to the PCC.

The Vicar may have been pleased to see an unprecedented number of young people at the annual meeting, but he was blissfully unaware of what they were up to. They were under strict orders to cast all their votes for others their age. When the votes were tallied, three prominent townspeople had lost their place on the PCC. Davison quickly realised who was responsible for this turn of events, and was not at all happy with Len!

According to the annual parochial meeting notes, 1937 saw the completion of the restorations begun the previous year and the construction of a new Church Hall on Hart Hill. Someone present at the meeting suggested that the Churchyard be *made more beautiful* by removing the historic tombstones. Thankfully members promptly vetoed the proposal.

Mr. William Bird, who had attended more than 2,000 weddings at St. Mary's, made local headlines when he died in January 1938.[73] The verger for 32 years, Mr. Bird prided himself on having never missed a wedding, christening or communion while he held the post. Davison eulogised Bird as an *ideal verger*.

"No one could have been more dignified, and he had just the right gait for the job," noted Davison. But the Vicar added that he could be a little intimidating to the brides and bridegrooms. "He was very independent in his treatment of them, and he almost frightened them off!"

Celebrating 800 years

While the 1,000th anniversary of Ethestan's church passed unobserved, the 800th birthday of the Earl of Gloucester's church suffered no such fate. In grand style, the celebration lasted from May 29 to June 5, 1938.

Brilliant sunlight greeted the Mayor and other officials when they left the Town Hall to march to St. Mary's for the anniversary service. The Bishop of St. Albans gave the address, noting that the church had become so much a part of daily life that people were apt to take it for granted. However, he went on to warn the congregation that *Christianity would only continue in this country if people were prepared to make those personal sacrifices of time, leisure, service, witness and material wealth by which it was first founded.*[74]

Another celebration followed on Wednesday evening, which included five hundred representatives from fifteen churches carved out of the original parish of Luton.

Live From St. Mary's

An unusually large crowd attended Choral Evensong on September 18th that year and afterwards people stayed for a special, second service. The BBC had come to broadcast a forty-five minute program, the first ever in St. Mary's history. The Vicar's message reflected that events leading up to World War II were reaching a critical point:

> I commend to you all this week and at all times that we should remember those who are working in the cause of peace. More things are done by prayer than this world dreams of.[75]

He went on to say that if the walls of St. Mary's could speak and express the feelings of the hundreds of thousands who had worshipped there, they would say that for the healing of men's souls there was nothing finer than the worship of God.

Rare is the occasion when people have to be kept *out* of the church, but such an event occurred during Harvest Festival Sunday in October 1938. Always a popular service, this particular one shattered the record. In spite of bringing in more chairs, the doors had to be shut fifteen minutes before the start of the service! The newspaper reported that *many people were unable to gain admission.*[76]

In March 1939, the well-loved Fred Gostelow celebrated his 50-year anniversary as organist of St. Mary's. To show their appreciation, the church presented him with an illuminated testimonial, now kept at the Bedfordshire County Archives and Records Service.

Luton expanded rapidly in the thirties, with people coming to work for such firms as Vauxhall and Electrolux. Soon a need for a daughter church arose in the area of St. Anne's Hill. Parishioners from St. Mary's raised the money for the new church through bazaars, donations and subscriptions. Later on, the Vicar introduced *Gift Days* to raise funds for necessary repairs to St. Mary's. The Gift Days remained an annual event from 1940 to 1960, when Canon Davison would stand in the north porch and receive donations from parishioners.

"It was all very necessary," said Davison, "and I am grateful to the many who responded, for as the years went on we assumed more and more responsibilities."[77]

The responsibilities Davison referred to were churches they were helping. When he arrived, they had only one: St. Mary's. When he retired, the number had grown to six: East Hyde, St. Paul's, Cockernhoe, St. Francis and St. Anne's.

War Hits Home

When England entered the Second World War, soldiers came to Luton for specialised training at Vauxhall; school children, evacuated from London came for safety reasons. Both these groups contributed to the rising attendance of the morning service. Because of the black out, attendance at Evensong fell. The 108 young people who had joined the services further reduced the evening congregation. One of these men was Len Ridd, who had to give up the PCC for the four years he was overseas.

During the war, Davison had the help of three curates who did double duty as Air Raid Wardens. Part of their responsibilities included supervising the fire-watching from their churches.

"From the roof of St. Mary's we could see the terrible fires of London, thirty miles away," Davison recalled.

In August 1940, stray bombs from an air raid on Vauxhall damaged the south transept of the church. They didn't hit St. Mary's directly, but fell on the Crawley Green Road Cemetary. The resulting blast was what caused the damage. Eighteen months later the church received a check for £47 from the War Damage Commission to pay for temporary repair work. The estimated cost of all the repairs came to about £400.[78]

On a Saturday morning early in June 1942, with the war still raging, the Revd William Davison was seen walking around town wearing a sandwich board! Nor was he alone. Ten other clergymen in the vicinity also sported the boards. But they were not proclaiming the end of the world; they were advertising something called *Religion and Life Week*.

The purpose of the event was to help people understand Christianity's relevance to every aspect of life, a concept that medieval parishioners had accepted without question. Five thousand people attended the opening service held on the town football ground Sunday evening, June 14th. Meetings at various churches throughout the week highlighted issues such as Marriage and Family, Education, Religion and Science, Commerce and Industry, and the Worldwide Church.

Sad Farewell

Parishioners attending church on Sunday, June 28th were stunned to hear that 75-year-old Fred Gostelow had died the previous evening. Gostelow enjoyed good health up until the hour he collapsed at home in a chair and died.

At the funeral, Canon Davison eulogized the musician as *more than an organist...He was a physician of the soul who loved the work of God and was loved by his pupils, by the congregation, his colleagues at Trinity College, and all the Vicars with whom he had worked.*[79]

Nearly everyone in Luton was familiar with Fred Gostelow. He had won the Heathcote Long prize in 1885 and a gold medal at the International Music Trades Exhibition in 1896. An examiner and professor of Trinity College of Music, he also composed anthems and songs for the church. For over thirty years he conducted the Luton Choral and Orchestral Society.

The people he had so faithfully served for fifty-three years established a scholarship fund in Gostelow's name and erected a brass plaque in the chancel to his memory.

While the war increased the clergy's workload, it made St. Mary's bell-ringers redundant because church bells were only to be rung in the extreme case of a German invasion. Winston Churchill made one exception, when the allies were victorious in North Africa. On this occasion he called for all the bells in Britain to ring out a thanksgiving peal.

Canon Davison noted that he had never seen so many people inside and outside the church as on this day. With every seat filled, people wedged themselves into the aisles and under the church tower. They flooded the churchyard as well. Impressed by the demonstration, Davison decided to restore the bells after the war as a sign of thanksgiving to God for His grace and care.

Last Sermon to the Nation
Dr. William Temple, the Archbishop of Canterbury, came to St. Mary's to preach a message for the National Day of Prayer in September 1944. With the help of the BBC, Dr. Temple's sermon was broadcasted all over the Empire:

> The first anniversary of our entry into the war was marked by deep anxiety controlled by firm resolve. Our sense of dependence on God was quickened by very present dangers...It is good for us to look back to those dark days and to remember through what perils the mercy of God sustained us. It gives more vividness to our thanksgivings as we meet today with high hopes, because we believe the end of the war is in sight...We look forward to victory as something within our grasp, and beyond victory to the use which should be made of it. We are not now concerned with the political arrangements which must be made, but with the spirit in which we shall enter upon the new era. For it must be a new era, otherwise we shall have failed.[80]

Less than two months later, Archbishop Temple died of a pulmonary embolism. He had preached his final sermon to the nation from St. Mary's.

At long last the war ended and Lutonians, including the Mayor and civil dignitaries, expressed their relief in a great service of thanksgiving at the Parish Church.

Canon Davison's inspiration to restore and rehang the bells became a reality in 1949. Two more bells were added, bringing the total to ten.

A surprising entry in the church's guest book on 15 August 1949, notes that the Archbishops of Canterbury and York were present for the 1,018th anniversary of the first stone church dedicated by King Ethelstan. No other record of this anniversary exists, not even in the newspapers. How an event with such esteemed personages could slip unnoticed by journalists is yet another mystery and casts doubt that it actually occurred.

Make Way for the Queen

If people crowded into the church for Harvest Festivals and the Archbishop of Canterbury, there was no less enthusiasm for Queen Elizabeth II when she and Prince Phillip, made their first visit to St. Mary's in November 1952. They had been staying at Luton Hoo for their anniversary. By 7 a.m. people were waiting in the pouring rain hoping for a seat when the doors opened three hours later. Canon Davison preached before her Majesty on seven such visits during his tenure. He confessed:

> At first I was nervous about the Royal visits. They were private affairs, but nonetheless, great preparation and precaution had to be made, and congregations often reached into the churchyard...Nearly all the members of the Royal Family came to our morning service at one time or another as well as the King and Queen of Sweden and Ambassadors of European and American Embassies.[81]

For some reason, parishioners in the 1990's believed that the squint hole[82] in the Wenlock Screen had been created for the benefit of the Queen when she began attending services. However, Cobbe mentions the squint hole in his book published in the 19th century, debunking the myth that it was added later. There is no reason to conclude other than it was a part of the original work, made in an era when the Elevation of the Host was the highlight of the service, and thus vital that the laity see it.

The Secretary of State bestowed a great honour on St. Mary's in 1954 by declaring it a Grade 1 Listed building. It is the only building in Luton with such a distinction. Although the majority of Anglican churches in England are listed, only two percent of all

Queen Elizabeth II with Canon Davison. Prince Phillip and Sir Harold Wernher are in the background.

listed buildings in the country are designated Grade 1. The 14th and 15th century character of the church, as well as the chequered stonework won over those in charge of the ratings. Today English Heritage is the government agency that protects historic buildings in England, including St. Mary's.

Although it must have been difficult to leave such a distinguished church after 28 years, Canon Davison retired from his post as Vicar in 1961. He had twice turned down an appointment in the Lake District because he felt he could do better work in Luton.

The Flying Vicar

Harold Frankham, a Lutonian and former curate at St. Mary's during World War II, succeeded Davison. Before his appointment as Vicar, he suffered paralysis from contracting polio. He later made what many considered a miraculous recovery after a clergyman with a reputed gift of healing laid hands on him and prayed. Like his predecessor, Harold Frankham would also go on to become Rural Dean and a Canon.

Len Ridd remembered the Vicar as a fine preacher who conducted beautiful services. "He came to Luton at a difficult time," Ridd acknowledged. "Few people in the congregation knew any Vicar before Davison and after 28 years, all of us had gotten into a certain way of doing things."

The Revd Harold Frankham

Frankham travelled frequently to the United States. In February 1963, he made his 17th trip across the Atlantic to conduct a Parish Mission in Toledo and lecture at Ohio State University at

Columbus. Regarding his lectures at the University, Frankham observed: "They were not a great deal interested in religion."

Cars, Vacuums, and Protests

Since St. Mary's had once housed three fire engines, perhaps it shocked no one to see a shiny new Vauxhall parked in the church. It all began in 1965 with an observation that the church celebrated annual Harvest Festivals though Luton was no longer an agricultural town. Why not hold an Industrial Festival?

The idea gathered momentum and the weekend before the Harvest Festival, various companies set up displays within the church, including Vauxhall, Electrolux, Napier Aviation and members of the hat-making industry. These "fruits of the factory" displayed in the church guaranteed the Festival a unique place in St. Mary's history.

Protests and sit-ins were a common occurrence in the sixties, so there was nothing unusual about 25 jean-clad young people sitting in the churchyard on a Saturday in May 1967. They were members of St. Mary's Youth Club on a 24-hour hunger strike to protest famine in the world. Aside from experiencing hunger, the youth collected donations for a Christian Aid project in Chile, which was reeling from one of the worst famines in the world at that time.

The new Church Hall came about during Frankham's tenure, but not without some strong disagreement from the congregation.

A number of parishioners opposed the site selected for the hall and signed a petition expressing their dismay. Two sites were originally considered: east of the chancel and the southwest corner of the churchyard. Those who supported the latter reasoned that putting a building on the east side would obstruct the view of the old church and produce an *unpleasant effect.*

In a letter to the Vicar, opponents informed him that even Sir Harold Wernher (owner of Luton Hoo) had described the project as outrageous. They also told Frankham that the Historic

Buildings Council opposed the idea, though it had no executive power. In the end, Frankham won out and the building found a place between the east end of the church and the street.

Dedication of the new hall was set for Saturday, 8 February 1969. The Bishop of St. Albans was present to perform his duties, but unfortunately, a blizzard prevented many of the 300 invited guests from attending.

A Sneeze that Almost Shattered Protocol

Frankham's era included other visits by the Queen, though the crowds lining up were smaller and waited only for a little more than an hour outside the church. The royal party also included Prince Phillip and Lord Mountbatten.

Towards the end of his time in Luton, Harold Frankham suggested that Len Ridd accept the nomination for churchwarden. Ridd agreed and held the position for two terms.

Ridd was churchwarden during one of her Majesty's visits and had the privilege of escorting the Queen to her seat in Wenlock Chapel.

"By that time we had all the arrangements down and were used to it. She always arrived exactly at six minutes to eleven o'clock," remembered Mr. Ridd.

"A delightful policeman came ahead of time and asked me if I could open the great west doors by myself. I told him I could, and then he inquired as to how I would know when the Queen was coming. There was a crack in the door through which I could see another constable outside. He arranged for that officer to pull his handkerchief from his trouser pocket when the Queen's car drew up to the gate. That would be my signal to open the doors."

Through the crack, Ridd kept his eye glued on the police officer. Suddenly the man reached for his handkerchief, and with adrenaline surging the Churchwarden flew into action.

"I swung the doors open just in time to see the policeman raise his handkerchief to his nose and sneeze into it! I had to quickly shut them again!"

After that false start, however, everything proceeded smoothly and Ridd escorted the Queen to her seat without incident.

He also recalled the occasions when Lady Wernher of Luton Hoo attended the service.

"We would get a phone call about 15 minutes before Matins...from her butler I guessed. 'Four from the Hoo in the Chapel,' he would announce, and we would know she was coming with guests. Her visits did not take the stage like the Queen's of course, but I always escorted her to the Wenlock Chapel."

When Frankham left St. Mary's in 1971, a dynamic young man named Christopher Mayfield took his place. It was his first post as Vicar, but what Mayfield lacked in experience he made up for with energy and vision. He set about equipping parishioners to *do the work of the ministry* and developed leaders from among the congregation.

The Revd Christopher Mayfield

Breaking Gender Barriers and Stained Glass

Len Ridd was in his last term as churchwarden when Mayfield arrived. In his final act as warden, Ridd broke the gender barrier by nominating the first sideswomen in the history of the church. Enid Pearce, the little girl who had presented a gift to the Revd R.T. Howard, was among this group of sideswomen. By this time she already held the distinction of being the first woman secretary of the Parochial Church Council. More importantly, she went on to become the first female churchwarden in the history of St. Mary's.

In 1976, Luton celebrated its 50th anniversary as an incorporated town. St. Mary's marked the event with a gospel rock concert in the churchyard. Although the entrance fee was a mere 35 pence, some of the rowdier fans tried to crash the concert without paying. Police were summoned to help the stewards at the gates. Inside the churchyard, hundreds sat peacefully on the grass or leaned against tombstones and listened to the *Fish Company*, a Christian rock group.

Curate Anthony Fletcher felt the event was a great success.[83] It certainly produced one of the more unusual sights in the churchyard!

Thieves violated St. Mary's yet again in 1976. Sometime after the Choral Evensong service on 4 July, the culprits smashed a stained glass window in the south transept. Entering through the opening, they managed to break into the strong room and steal more than £3,000 of silver and pewter objects, as well as an electric typewriter and a cassock. Presumably they used the cassock to carry away the plunder. It was the largest theft in St. Mary's history. The criminals got away with three pewter plates, a silver George III alms dish, a silver processional cross, a silver altar cross in Gothic style, a silver altar cross in Renaissance style, two silver candlesticks, and two silver-plated flower vases.[84]

Apprentices and staff of Vauxhall Motors later presented the church with a cross and set of candlesticks made from stainless steel to replace those stolen.

Sleeping with the Silver

An eight-day Flowers and Arts Festival attracted large numbers to the church in the summer of 1979. Organised by the congregation, Chris Mayfield pointed out that the purpose was not so much to raise funds as to share the Good News. Approximately 200 people from St. Mary's planned and carried out the event. Over 3,000 visited the Festival, which included an exhibition of lace making, hat making, artwork, pewter, engraved glasswork, photography and brass rubbing. According to Mayfield, the Festival stirred a lot of interest in the church.

The public would have been even more curious had they been aware that certain members of the congregation were sleeping with the church silver that week. A number of valuable items were on display at the festival, including the 1610 communion cup normally kept in a bank vault. Clive Richardson, the verger, joined the rota of men who alternated sleeping with guarding the valuables. Although the experience couldn't have been too comfortable, Richardson remembers it as being rather enjoyable.

The night watch recalled the occasion when men in the 15th century guarded the silver pyx in the Easter Sepulchre.

In 1979, the Barnard Chantry gained a wrought iron grill– a gift of The Friends of Luton Parish Church. A charitable organisation established in 1965, The Friends help raise funds for maintaining the fabric of St. Mary's. From their beginning until the close of the century, this vital charity gave the church over £300,000 for restorations, improvements and repairs.

Also in 1979, a new stained glass window known as the Magnificat was installed in the south transept to replace the old one damaged by vandalism. Five artists had been invited to submit abstract designs on the theme of the Magnificat. Alan Younger won the commission with a window design that suggested *Mary's explosion of happiness and outpouring of gratitude.*

In December of that year, St. Mary's said goodbye to Chris Mayfield, who became the Archdeacon of Bedford and later the Bishop of Manchester.

New Roles for Women

Changes in the Anglican Church in the seventies permitted women to train for ministry and join the ranks of the clergy. Luton-born Janet Birch, who had attended St. Mary's since the

1940's, became the church's first female clerical staff member. Her role as deaconess was a full-time, non-stipendiary position with responsibilities similar to an assistant curate.

Birch began her groundbreaking role in 1980, and was well received by the congregation.

"I was terrified going into it and wondered how people would feel, but everybody was supportive and friendly," remembered Birch. "Some of the people I trained with were not as well received. It helped that I was already a member of the church."

Not all of Mrs. Birch's experiences were smooth, however. She remembered leading the funeral service of a well-known person and feeling a bit intimidated by the predominately male congregation.

"They were looking quite aghast at the thought of a woman taking the service, but afterwards they seemed satisfied with how it turned out."

In 1987, Janet Birch accepted a stipendiary post at St. Margaret's, Streatley. Once again, she became the first woman clergy on staff, but found people there supportive as well.

To mark the 850th anniversary, St. Mary's Players put on a drama pageant depicting the history of the church throughout the centuries. Thelma Shacklady and Chris Barnes wrote the script and Len Ridd produced it. The Pageant took place over a week in November 1987, and highlighted major events at St. Mary's and in the town.

History of another kind occurred in 1988 when Susie and Rod Sanders joined the staff as the church's first ordained couple. They were ordained as deacons together that year at St. Albans Cathedral. Rod was ordained a priest the following year, but since the Church had not yet extended that opportunity to women, Susie was unable to join him.

"It felt odd, since up to that time we had done everything together," she noted.

However, the Sanders were still at St. Mary's when the General Synod passed the measure allowing the ordination of women as priests. She remembers watching the debate and vote at home on television with other members of the staff.

The Revds Rod and Susie Sanders. Mrs. Sanders was St. Mary's first woman priest.

"When I went to the supermarket in my clerical collar later that day, all sorts of people came up to wish me well. Only one or two said things like, 'Oh, you're...one of them!' I did have a few instances where people asked not to be married by a woman, but they were offset by those who particularly requested me to take their services."

Changes in the Spiritual Climate

David Banfield was St. Mary's Vicar when the Sanders were curates. Mrs. Sanders remembers him as a gentle and prayerful man. Banfield inherited an active, enthusiastic congregation from his predecessor. The choir was as popular as ever and an outreach to the parents of choristers who accompanied their children to church. But church attendance in England was declining, the population of the town was changing, and entertainment choices were numerous. There were other spiritual options as well, some of them alarming. People no longer looked to the Church to provide answers or meet their social needs.

The Revd David Banfield

A Pastor's Heart

David Banfield left the church in 1991, and the honour of leading St Mary's through the last decade of the century and into a new millennium fell to the Revd Nicholas Bell, B.Sc.

Bell grew up in a working class neighbourhood of Oxford, which like Luton had a car manufacturing plant. As a young man, he attended a church in the town centre and went to the Cathedral Choir School. The new Vicar seemed custom designed for ministry at St. Mary's.

When Bell first arrived, the staff at St. Mary's consisted only of ordained clergy. Holding the biblical view that all Christians are called to minister, he set about to enlarge and diversify the team. Eventually, it included a mix of ordained and non-ordained members.

The Revd Nicholas Bell

Mr. Bell's first year at the church coincided with the induction of Luton's first Asian Mayor, Mr. Mick Guha. In the past, St. Mary's Vicar functioned as the Mayor's chaplain, but Mr. Guha was Hindu. As a public servant, he represented a plurality of religions and felt that leaders from different faiths should share the responsibility of opening council meetings with prayer.

The traditional civic service marking a new mayor's term was also about to change. Mr. Guha requested an inter-faith service. Bell did not feel in good conscience that he could allow St. Mary's to host such an event. The Bishop overruled, and in June 1991 the service took place. It was a low point for the Vicar, but to his relief, the event has never been repeated. The next mayor dispensed with the service entirely.

In spite of their different beliefs, the Vicar and Mr. Guhu liked and respected each other. When the Mayor's term ended, Mr. Bell wrote a public letter of thanks to Guhu for his leadership, remarking that

> Mayor Mick has worked tirelessly to bring together the many disparate groupings within the town and wherever he has been he has shown interest, courtesy, grace and humour.[85]

If the Revd James O'Neill was known as the "galloping Vicar," then his twentieth century counterpart could easily be dubbed the "running Vicar." A member of the St. Alban's Striders, Mr. Bell was a marathoner who raised money for charity by running in the famous London Marathon.

One of the Vicar's priorities was to get the church more involved in evangelism. In 1995 St. Mary's began offering the highly successful Alpha Course. The 10-week program presented the gospel in a no-pressure environment where people voiced their questions and doubts about Christianity. By the end of the decade, St. Mary's had run a total of nine courses which according to the Vicar, resulted in a number of transformed lives and brought people into the church.

Parishioners have been impressed by Nick Bell's pastoral heart and desire to see people changed and healed.

"Of all the Vicars I've known, Nick is the most gifted pastor," said Len Ridd, who retired from the PCC in 1993 after serving 50 years. "He has a great pastoral gift and really wants to help people."

Changes and Challenges

Regardless of his love for people, no pastor escapes criticism or misunderstanding. Struggle and grief came unexpectedly for the

Vicar in an area that had been a source of pride – the choir. Initially, Bell was excited about coming to a church with such a reputable music program. But there were several problems he had not anticipated.

Boys singing in the services had to miss Sunday School. Sometimes the 40-voice choir outnumbered the congregation attending the evening service, creating an awkward situation. And while the choir had earlier fulfilled an evangelistic function, this was no longer the case.

To complicate the situation, a rapid succession of music directors came and went for various reasons. Finally, unable to find a suitable director, the Vicar reluctantly gave the choir a sabbatical. This agonising decision drew heated criticism. The majority of the congregation, as well as Bell, hoped that a choir would be re-established in the future.

Another tradition to undergo radical surgery was the Evensong service. Nick Bell laboured to make St. Mary's a contemporary church. In the age of Internet and extreme music styles, younger people could not relate to Latin choral chants, so the service was overhauled. Robes, ruffled collars, and pipe organ gave way to t-shirts, drums, and electric guitars. St. Mary's was learning to speak Christianity in the language of another generation, and as a result attendance increased significantly.

Long-standing members of the congregation have not always found the changes easy to accept. Some are deeply pained, while others like Enid Pearce are more philosophical.

"I'm conservative," she admits. "But I've learned that it's only by accepting change that the church can continue; otherwise it dies. Although I can just endure the evening service, when you remember that sometimes there were only six people in the congregation and you see it now, you can only rejoice."

In the latter half of the decade, Churchwarden Richard Birchall became concerned over the state of the church's inventory. Churchwardens are responsible for maintaining the inventories, and in such an ancient church, the job can be rather daunting. Birchall decided that St. Mary's could use some expert help and after getting Mr. Bell's and the Archdeacon of Bedford's approval, he turned to the National Association of Decorative and Fine Arts Societies. Church Recording is a section of the Societies, and in 1998 a team of Recorders began their work at St. Mary's. Under the leadership of Anne Thompson, the recorders made detailed notes and photographs of the church's memorials, metal work (including silver and armour), flower vases, stonework, woodwork, paintings, textiles, library, windows and other miscellaneous objects. Their painstaking work would take three years and upon completion, the results would be sent to English Heritage, the County Record Office, the Council for the Care of Churches and the Victorian and Albert Museum.

The Secret of the Armour

Through the efforts of the Church Recorders a fascinating discovery came to light regarding the two armoured helmets that were mounted in the Wenlock Chapel at it's restoration in 1915. Tradition held that the armour belonged to Lord Wenlock, founder of the Chapel. Barbara and Simon Cotton, the Recorders assigned to the metal work, contacted the Royal Armouries in order to verify the dates of the helmets.

The results surprised everyone. The larger of the two helmets was actually made up from a number of pieces from various periods, all of which post-date Lord Wenlock. Thom Richardson of the Royal Armouries suggested that it was actually a *funeral helmet*.

"Helmets were often placed on church walls above tombs as part of what were called *achievements*," says Richardson. "All of the pieces of armour were carried before the bier in the funeral procession before being deposited in the church. This practice was common in England from the mid-fourteenth to the mid-seventeenth century."

Because the latest piece of the helmet is from the 17th century, it possibly belonged to one of the Rotherhams or Crawleys. Both families had rights to the chapel and were buried there. Because the families were also linked by the marriage of Sir Francis Crawley to Elizabeth Rotherham, theoretically the armour could have from ancestors on both sides. Sir Francis and Lady Crawley both died in the mid-1600's.

The mysterious armoured helmets that hung in the Wenlock Chapel for nearly a century

The second armoured helmet dated from approximately 1620, so could not have belonged to Lord Wenlock either. It does not appear to have been for funereal purposes, and its history remains a mystery. Extensive damage to the skull of the helmet could explain the demise of the owner.

As the 20th century drew to a close, St. Mary's joined forces with Stopsley Baptist Church and Luton Christian Fellowship to sponsor a Millennium Conference. Held the third week of October, the Conference emphasised the task of evangelism in the next century. Stuart and Jill Briscoe, an internationally acclaimed husband and wife team, were the Conference speakers.

The theme of the Conference fit perfectly with the vision Nick Bell and the congregation have for St. Mary's.

"Our desire is that St. Mary's will be a beacon for Christ," explains the Vicar. "We want people to know we are here and that they can come as they are and find love and acceptance."

Armistice Day 1999 marked a special celebration for St. Mary's and the University of Luton. The University, which holds its graduation ceremonies in St. Mary's, had the tower clock restored as a millennium gift to the church and people of Luton. Originally installed in 1901, the clock ceased chiming in '71. It remained silent for 28 years until the dedication ceremonies on 11 November.

St. Mary's had their own gift to present the people of Luton: a Millennium Flame symbolising 2,000 years of the Light and Love of Christ. In view of the congregation's desire to be a beacon for Christ, it seemed a fitting gift. As church bells chimed in the New Millennium, a town councillor threw the switch and lit the three-tiered flame. Lutonians gathered in front of Town Hall for the occasion, cheered and burst into a chorus of Auld Lang Syne.

Over 860 New Years have come and gone since parishioners first gathered within the walls of St. Mary's. More than just an impressive building, the church has been a stage where men and women acted out the spectrum of their humanity. Each generation wove their threads of greatness and failure into the tapestry of her life and created a resplendent past. Luton has every right to be proud of St. Mary's. Few parish churches can match the history and beauty of this Medieval Jewel.

Appendix A

My Love Mourneth

by Vicar John Gwynneth
   (published in 1530)

And I mankind have not in mind
My love that mourneth for me, for me,
Who is my love but God above
That born was of Mary. And on the rode
His precious blood He shed to make me free.
Whom should I prove so true of love
So gentle and courteous as he.

The Father his son from heaven sent down
And born was of a maid.
The prophesy of Isaiah fulfilled he and said,
Behold mankind, thy Maker most loving
For thy love come to die.
What is thy mind to be so unkind, sayeth I
So mourn for thee, for thee.

That virgin's child most meek and mild
Alonely for my sake his Father's will for to fulfill
He came great pains to take
And suffered death as Scripture sayeth
That we should saved be on Good Friday.
Wherefore I say, he mourned for me, for me.

Such pain and smart as in his heart
He suffered for mankind.

Can no man take nor mourning make
So meekly for his friend.
The cruel Jews would not refuse
To nail him to a tree
And with a dart to pierce his heart
Thus mourned he for me.

Now Christ Jesus of Love most true
Have mercy upon me.
I asketh grace for my trespass
That I have done to thee.
For thy sweet name save me from shame
And all adversity.
For Mary's sake to thee me take
And mourn no more for me.

Appendix B

St. Mary's Rectors and Vicars

RECTORS	DATE	PATRON
Morcar the Saxon	1050	Edward the Confessor
William the Chamberlain	1086	William the Conqueror
William the Younger	1135	Earl Robert of Gloucester
Gilbert de Cymmay	1139	
		Robert de Waudari
RECTORS VICAR		
Geoffrey de Gorham	1153	William, Earl of Gloucester
Balderic de Sigillo		King Henry II
Adam the Clerk		Abbot of St. Albans
TEMPORARY VICAR		
Mag. Roger de Luton	1197	
PERPETUAL VICARS		
Mag. John de St. Albans	1219	
Adam de Biscot	1227	
Henry	1248	
Geoffrey	1248	
Roger de Mursle	1275	
Hugh de Baneburgh	1276	
John de Wilden	1316	
Robert de Wyboldeston	1321	
Roger de Salesbury	1321	
John de Standfordham	1331	
Dom John Rasen de Luton	1346	

VICARS	DATE	PATRONS
Mag. Andrew Power de Mentmore	1349	
Dom Richard de Rochele	1349	
William de Chaumbre de St. Neots	1350	King Edward III
John Lybert	1353	Abbot of St. Albans
Mag. Walter Ixworth		
Mag. John Peche	1393	
Mag. John Blomham	1413	
Mag. John Penthelyn		Abbot of St. Albans
Mag. Roger Burgh	1444	
Mag. John Lammer	1454	
Mag. Richard Barnard	1147	
Adrian Castello	1492	
Mag. Edward Sheffield	1502	Sir Robert Sheffield
Richard Doke	1526	Cardinal Wolsey
Mag. Thomas Heritage	1526	
John Gwynneth	1537	
George Mason	1558	Queen Elizabeth I
Thomas Rose	1562	
William Horne	1575	
Edmund Brockett	1593	King James I
John Birde	1617	
		Sir Robert Napier
INTRUDED MINISTERS		
Samuel Austin	1645	
Thomas Atwood Rotherham	1646	
Mr. Carey	1647	
Thomas Jessop	1650	
Thomas Pomfret	1660	Sir Robert Napier
Christopher Eaton	1646	Sir John Napier
George Barnard	1745	Sir John Napier (Jr.)

VICARS	DATE	PATRONS
William Prior	1760	Francis Herne
The Hon. William Stuart	1779	John 3rd Earl of Bute
James Russell Deare	1795	King George III
Stuart Corbett	1798	John, 1st Marquess of Bute
Charles Henry Hall	1804	
Hon. Canon William McDouall	1827	
Thomas Sikes	1850	John Sikes and John Burder
Thomas Bartlett	1854	Rev. Alex. King
Thomas W. Peile	1857	William Robinson, Esq.
George Quirk	1861	John Foster Baird, Esq.
James O'Neill	1862	James O'Neill
Hon. Canon Edmund Mason	1897	The Peache Trustees
Arthur Chapman	1911	
Hon. Canon C. Mollan Williams	1921	
Richard T. Howard	1929	
Hon. Canon William Davison	1933	
Hon. Canon Harold Frankham	1961	
Christopher Mayfield	1971	
Hon. Canon David Banfield	1980	
Nicholas Bell	1991	

Photographic Acknowledgements

The author wishes to thank the following for permission to reproduce their photographs: Eric Meadows – pages 15, 21, 30, 39, 52, 142, 147; Luton Museum Service – pages 42, 44, 45, 120; The Luton News, courtesy of Luton Museum Service – pages 138, 139, 146; by permission of the British Library, the photo of Archbishop Thomas Rotherham (shelfmark 10352.m.1) – page 43; The Representative Church Body Library, Dublin, RCB Library Portfolio of Portraits Volume 2, for the picture of Archbishop William Stuart - page 96; Bedfordshire and Luton Archives and Record Service (Luton St. Mary's collection) – pages 90, 109, 117, 124, 126, 127, 130; and Susie Sanders – page 146.

Notes

[1] Luton was called a Royal town of the British in the Saxon Chronicles of 571 AD. Under British, Saxon and Norman Kings, the town was the private property of the Crown, until it was given by Henry the First, early in the twelfth century, to his son Robert, Earl of Gloucester.
[2] *The Ecclesiastical History of the English People* by Bede, Oxford University Press, pp. 144 - 145
[3] The King's bailiff was the most important person in Luton, followed by a thane who owned Biscot. This particular thane would have been a soldier companion to the King. After the Conquest, the term referred to a freeman who ranked just below a nobleman.
[4] The Domesday Book
[5] The Tower of Tewkesbury Abbey was built by Robert and still stands. It is one of the largest surviving Norman towers in England today.
[6] Examples of these pilgrim badges are on display at the Luton Museum.
[7] From a deed written in November 1257 and preserved in the British Museum.
[8] *The History of Luton and its Hamlets* by William Austin, Vol. II p. 301
[9] The "d." was an abbreviation for penny, while "s." stood for shilling.
[10] Bedfordshire Wills Vol. 38, Bedfordshire Record Office
[11] A pax was a small plate with a handle on the back and on the front an image depicting the crucifixion.
[12] The pyx was a covered container used for holding the consecrated host.
[13] A sacristan is a church officer who has charge of the sacred utensils.
[14] Bedfordshire Wills vol. 38, Bedfordshire Record Office
[15] A plate on which the host was placed after it was taken from the pyx.
[16] The Sedilia is a set of seats used at the Mass by the priest, deacon and sub deacon. St. Mary's sedilia is unusual as it contains a fourth seat, possibly for the Abbot.
[17] Chantries were chapels endowed for saying daily Masses for the soul of the founder and the souls of others he designated.
[18] A deposit for relics.
[19] Described in an article by E. Craven Lee in *The Luton News and Bedfordshire Advertiser*, December 27, 1917.
[20] *Luton Church* by Henry Cobbe M.A., George Bell and Sons, 1899, p.169

[21] Edward Steele, a visitor to the church in the early 18th century, describes seeing this brass in the Nave, where it was originally located.
[22] *Luton Church* by Henry Cobbe M.A. p. 183 ...The author failed to site the original source of the quote.
[23] This book was on display in the British Museum in the 1800's and is now preserved in the British library. It was published October 10, 1530, although the editor and printer are not given.
[24] Transubstantiation is the doctrine that says the bread and wine used in the Eucharist is changed into the actual body and blood of Christ.
[25] A Declaration by John Gwynneth, p.ii (1554) Londini.
[26] Ibid.
[27] The noble was worth six shilling and eight pence.
[28] *History of a Bedfordshire Family* by William Austin, Alston Rivers, Ltd. 1911, p. 69-70.
[29] He died before 13 May 1559 as records tell us that a successor at Stotesbury, Northamptonshire (one of his preferments) was instituted "on the decease of the last incumbent."
[30] Foxe's early editions were entitled *Acts and Monuments of these latter and perillous dayes touching matters of the Church...* London, 1596; Vol. VIII; Pages 581-590 British Library (4824.K.4).
[31] *A Christian Exercise, Containing an easie entrance into the principles of religion, and the chiefest points of our salvation in Christe, with a direction for all Christians, into the true service of God.* By W. Horne, at London, Printed by Robert Walde-grave, dwelling without Temple-barre, neere unto Sommerset house. 3505.C.52.
[32] The precise dates between Camden's visit to Luton and the repair of the roof are debatable and vary depending on which source you read.
[33] The *History and Antiquities of the Chapel at Luton Park* by Henry Shaw L.P. London, 1830.
[34] State Papers, Domestic Interregnum, vol. clxxxi. No. 59.
[35] The sermon, delivered September 9th at Ampthill. A published copy exists in the British Library.
[36] This was noted by Mr. A. Humphreys, Rector of Barton in Bedfordshire, in his sermon preached at Pomfret's funeral. A copy of the sermon can be found in the British Library (1418.f.1.)
[37] *The History of Luton and its Hamlets* by William Austin, Vol. II., p.63
[38] John Marten, Librarian at Woburn Abbey (1845-1854). This gallery was constructed in 1721.

[39] *The Northampton Mercury*, 22 November 1747.
[40] The Journal of John Wesley, Thursday, 16 January 1771.
[41] From a letter to Lady Charlotte Finch from George III at Windsor, dated July 13th, 1800. Reprinted in *Stuartiana or Bubbles blown by and to some of the family of Stuart*, 1857. British Library, shelfmark C.193.b.26
[42] ibid
[43] *Three Sermons Preached at the Spring, Summer and First Winter Assizes*, for the county of Kent, 1822; before the High Sheriff, John Powell, Esq. His majesty's judges of Assize by James Russell Deare, L.L. B., Vicar of Bures, in the county of Suffolk; chaplain in ordinary to his Majesty; and, on the above-mentioned occasions, to the High Sheriff.
[44] *Gentleman's Magazine* was founded in 1731 by Edward Cave and included literary criticism, essays and parliamentary reports. It is thought to be the first publication to use the term *magazine*.
[45] *The Pictorial*, August 16, 1966, p.5.
[46] By John Marten, Librarian of Woburn Abbey and published in *The Northampton Mercury*, 27 February 1847.
[47] *The Changing Face of Luton*, by Stephen Bunker, Robin Holgate and Marian Nichols, The Book Castle, 1993, p.89.
[48] *Bedford Times*, 11 September 1860.
[49] *The Luton Times*, September 8, 1860.
[50] *The Luton Times and Dunstable Herald*, Saturday, February 22, 1862.
[51] *The Luton Times and Dunstable Herald*, February 1, 1862.
[52] *The Luton Times and Dunstable Herald*, May 10, 1862.
[53] *History of the Various Restorations of the Parish Church of Luton*, by the Revd James O'Neill, B.D. 1888.
[54] *The Bedfordshire Advertiser*, Friday, January 1, 1897.
[55] Ibid.
[56] *The Luton Times and Dunstable Herald*, August 3, 1867.
[57] Ibid.
[58] *The Luton Times and Dunstable Herald*, Saturday, June 15, 1867.
[59] *The Bedfordshire Advertiser*, Friday, January 1, 1897.
[60] The Peache Trustees, a group of mostly clergymen, acquired the patronage of various livings which permitted them to appoint the incumbents.
[61] From a letter written by Revd E.R. Mason, Orton Vicarage, Southweel, to Mr. Tydeman on March 10, 1897, relating to residential accommodation, Bedfordshire County Archives and Record Service (P/ 85/28/2/11).

[62] Bedfordshire County Archives and Record Service (P/85/2/12/5).
[63] *The Bedfordshire Advertiser*, April 15, 1897.
[64] Bedfordshire County Archives and Record Service, (P 85/2/4/21).
[65] Bedfordshire County Archives and Record Service (P85/2/4/28).
[66] *Bedfordshire Advertiser and Luton Times*, November 14, 1907
[67] Bedfordshire County Archives and Record Service (P85/28/2/17).
[68] *The Bedfordshire Advertiser and Luton Times*, August 14, 1914.
[69] The Parvise or room above the south porch was at one time used as a museum for the church's artefacts.
[70] *The Luton News and Bedfordshire Advertiser*, November 8, 1917.
[71] *The Luton News and Bedfordshire Advertiser*, September 24, 1931.
[72] *The Luton News*, Thursday, July 2, 1942, page 6.
[73] *The Luton News*, Thursday, January 6, 1938.
[74] *The Luton News*, June 2, 1938.
[75] *The Luton News & Bedfordshire Advertiser*, September 2, 1938.
[76] *The Luton News & Bedfordshire Advertiser*, October 6, 1938.
[77] *Bedfordshire Magazine*, Vol. XVI, No. 121, page 94.
[78] *The Luton News*, April 16, 1942.
[79] *The Luton News*, July 2, 1942.
[80] *The Luton News*, September 7, 1944.
[81] *Bedfordshire Magazine*, Vol. XVI, no. 121, page 143.
[82] Squint Holes, a medieval contrivance, were carved into wood and stone screens to allow the laity to see the elevation of the host.
[83] *The Luton News*, June 3, 1976.
[84] *The Luton News*, July 8, 1976.
[85] *The Luton News & Dunstable Gazette*, June 3, 1992

Index

Acworth, John, *42*, 54
Advowson, 12, 13, 15, 16, 74, 102, 103, 106, 109, 117
Alhmund, 10
Anniversary Services, 129, 132, 133, 136, 143, 145
Attwood, Thomas, 73
Austin,
   Samuel, 77
   William, 87
Banfield, Revd David, 146, 147
Baptistry, 30, 92, 98, 99, 101, 109
Barber,
   John, 53
   Robert, 72
Barnard,
   Revd George, 88, 90, 144
   Richard, 48, 49
Bartlett, Revd Thomas, 103
Basley, Revd Daniel, 97
BBC, 132, 136
Bedfordshire, 8, 46, 76, 77, 101, 129
Bell, Revd Nicholas, 147, 149
Bidding of the bedes, 35
Birch, Janet, 144, 145
Bird, William, 131
Birde, John, 73, 74, 75, 76, 77
Biscot, 12, 15, 40, 54, 72

Blomham, John, 35
Boleyn, Sir Godfey, 46
Book of Sports, 74, 77
Boswell, James, 92
Brett, John, 98
Brocket, Edmund, 70, 73
Burgh, Revd Robert, 39
Bute Gallery, 104
Carey, Mr., 78
Castello, Adrian, 49, 50, 51, 56
Chapman, Revd Arthur E., 124, 125, 126
Charles I, 75, 77
Charles II, 82, 83
Cheney, Thomas, 83
Church galleries, 87
Church Missionary Society, 109, 127
Cobbe, Revd Henry, 111
Cockernhoe, 133
Cole, William, 91
Committee for Plundered Ministers, 77
Committee for Scandalous or Malignant Ministers, 76
Cooke, Harold, 127
Copleston, Coriolanus, 90, 97
Copt Hall, 92, 100
Corbet, Stuart, 97

Cranmer, Archbishop, 60, 65, 66
Crawley,
   Edward, 61
   J.S., 112
   John, 62
   Richard, 68
   Sir Francis, 74, 75, 76, 79, 151
   Thomas, 53, 74
Crawley, Lady
   burial of, 79
Cromwell,
   Oliver, 80
   Thomas, 55, 65
Crosse, Thomas, 83
Dallow, 10, 11
Danelaw, 10
Davison, Revd William, 130, 131, 133, 134, 135, 136, 137, 139
de Baneburgh, Hugh, 22
de Bethune, Baldwin, 17, 19
de Biscot, Adam, 21, 22
de Breauté, Falk, 19, 20
de Chaumbre, William, 26, 30
de Cymmay, Gilbert, 13, 15
de Gorham, Abbot Robert, 15, 16
de Luton,
   John, 26
   Roger, 18
de Mentmore, Andrew Power, 26
de Montfort, Simon, 22, 23
de Mursle, Roger, 22
de Rochele, Richard, 26

de Salesbury, Roger, 25
de Sigillo, Balderic, 16
de St. Alban, John, 20, 116
de Standfordham, John, 25
de Wilden, John, 25
Deare, Revd James Russell, 95
Doke, Richard, 55
Earl of Bute, John, 90, 92
East Hyde, 100, 133
Easter Sepulchre, 30, 144
Eaton, Revd Christopher, 88
Edward III, 26
Edward IV, 41, 42
Edward the Confessor, 10
Edward VI, 61
Elizabeth I, 63
Elizabeth II, 137, 141
English Heritage, 139
Ethelstan, 13, 18, 129, 136
Flowers and Arts Festival, 143
Forgotten tithes, 53
Foxe's Book of Martyrs, 64
Frankham, Revd Harold, 139, 140, 141, 142
Friends of Luton Parish Church, 144
Gentleman's Magazine, 95, 98
Geoffrey the Priest, 16
George III, 90, 95
Gloucester,
   Robert Earl of, 12, 116
   William Earl of, 16

Gostelow, Fred, 115, 130, 133, 135
Gough, Robert, 88
Grey, Edmund Earl of Kent, 46
Guha, Mayor Mick, 147
Guild of the Holy Trinity, 42, 46, 53, 61, 68
Gwynneth, John, 56, 58, 59, 60, 61, 62, 63, 66, 68, 109
Hall, Revd Charles Henry, 97, 100
Harvest festivals, 129, 133
Hay, John, 39, 46
Henry I, 12
Henry II, 16
Henry the Priest, 22
Henry VI, 40
Henry VII, 49
Henry VIII, 55, 60, 61, 62, 64, 66
Herytage, Thomas, 55, 56
Hoo Chapel, 46, 73, 74, 98, 102, 125
Horne, William, 68, 70
Howard, Revd Richard Thomas, 127, 128, 129
Howe, William, 72
Humphrey, Mr. A., 85, 86
Indulgences, 16
Ixworth, Mag. Walter, 30
James I, 73
Jessop, Thomas, 79, 81
Knight, Daniel, 89
Lammer, John, 39, 42
Leicester, 9

Luton Hoo, 70, 73, 74, 79, 82, 90, 102, 125, 140, 142
Lybert, John, 26, 30
Marquess of Bute, 100
Marsom, Samuel, 89, 90
Mason,
  Revd Edmund R., 117, 119, 121, 123, 124
  Revd George, 63, 64
Mayfield, Revd Christopher, 142, 143, 144
McDouall, Revd William, 100, 102
Mercia, 8, 9
Mission Church, the, 128
Morcar the Priest, 10, 11
Napier,
  Robert, 73, 74
  Robert Jr., 75, 76, 77, 79, 82
  Sir John, 84, 87, 88, 90
National Association of Decorative and Fine Arts Societies, 150
O'Neill, Revd James, 109, 110, 111, 112, 113, 114, 115, 116, 117, 123, 127
Offa, 10, 12
Oliver, Samuel, 112, 113, 114
Paeda, 8
Pax, 33, 61
Peache Trustees, 117
Peche, Revd John, 30, 32, 33
Peile, Dr. Thomas, 104, 106, 107

Pembroke, Eleanor Countess of, 22
Penn,
    Sophia Margaret, 93
    William, 93
Penthelyn, John, 36, 37, 38, 39
Plundered Ministers, 76, 77, 79
Pomfret,
    John, 82, 83
    Thomas, 82, 84, 86, 87
Pope Leo X, 49
Prior, Revd William, 90, 92
Puritans, 74, 77, 84
Pyx, 33, 34, 61, 144
Quirk, Revd George, 107, 108, 114
Ramridge, Abbot Thomas, 49
Reformation, 75, 90
Religion and Life Week, 134
Repton, 90, 92
Richard II, 27
Richard the Lionheart, 17
Rose, Thomas, 64, 65, 66, 67, 68, 94
Rotherham,
    Alice, 48
    Archbishop Thomas, 42, 48
    Elizabeth, 151
    John, 42, 48, 73, 74
    Sir Thomas, 52
    Thomas Atwood, 78
Rye House plot, 83
Sanders, Rod and Susie, 145

Sheffield, Edward, 51, 52, 53, 55
Sikes, Revd Thomas, 102, 103
Smith, John, 115
Someries (Wenlock) Chapel, 40, 74, 88
Spitele, John, 35, 36, 37
St. Alban's, 10, 12, 15, 16, 17, 20, 26, 27, 28, 34, 49, 55, 70, 83, 84, 145
St. Anne's, 119, 133
St. Francis, 133
St. Mary's Players, 128, 130
St. Nicholas Chapel, 75
St. Paul's, Luton, 133
Stocks in the churchyard, 56, 64, 88
Street, G.E., 110
Stuart,
    Lord Mount, 95
    William, 92, 93, 95, 98
Sylam, John, 54
Temple, Dr. William, 136
Tewkesbury Abbey, 14, 41, 122
Tewkesbury, battle of, 41, 74
Thieves, 23, 99, 105, 143
Vicarage, 20, 88, 100, 103, 117, 119, 123, 128
Victoria, Queen, 104
Washington, Lawrence, 81
Wells, Bishop Hugh, 20
Wenlock Chapel, 36, 38, 39, 48, 52, 75, 101, 121, 126, 141, 142
Wenlock Screen, 29

Wenlock,
    Elizabeth, 40
    Sir John, 36, 38, 39, 40, 41, 42, 46, 74, 116
    William, 28, 29, 30, 36, 39
Wernher,
    Lady, 125, 142
    Sir Harold, 140
    Sir Julius, 126
Wesley, John, 91
Wheathamstead, Abbot, 36, 37, 39, 55

William the Chamberlain, 11, 12, 13, 74
William the Conqueror, 11, 19
Williams, Revd Charles Mollan, 126, 127
Wingate, George, 72
Wolsey, Cardinal Thomas, 55
Wulfhere, 9, 12
Wyboldeston, Robert, 25
Wycliffe, John, 27, 28, 36, 37
Yardley, William, 98